Contents

Page references are to the Picador edition of *On the Black Hill* but as references are also given to particular chapters, the Notes may be used with any edition of the book.

Ellie

General editor: Graham Handley MA PhD

Brodie's Notes on Bruce Chatwin's

On the Black Hill

Philip Gooden BA
English Department, Kingswood School, Bath

Pan Books London, Sydney and Auckland

Extracts from *On the Black Hill*
by permission of the author and Jonathan Cape Ltd

First published 1988 by Pan Books Ltd,
Cavaye Place, London SW10 9PG
9 8 7 6 5 4 3 2 1

ISBN 0 330 50271 9
Photoset by Parker Typesetting Service, Leicester
Printed and bound in Great Britain by
Richard Clay Ltd, Bungay, Suffolk

Preface

The intention throughout this study aid is to stimulate and guide, to encourage the reader's *involvement* in the text, to develop disciplined critical responses and a sure understanding of the main details in the chosen text.

Brodie's Notes provide a summary of the plot of the play or novel followed by act, scene or chapter summaries, each of which will have an accompanying critical commentary designed to emphasize the most important literary and factual details. Poems, stories or non-fiction texts will combine brief summary with critical commentary on either individual aspects or sequences of the genre being considered. Textual notes will be explanatory or critical (sometimes both), defining what is difficult or obscure on the one hand, or stressing points of character, style, plot or the technical aspects of poetry on the other. Revision questions will be set at appropriate points to test the student's careful application to the text of the prescribed book.

The second section of each of these study aids will consist of a critical examination of the author's art. This will cover such major elements as characterization, style, structure, setting, theme(s) for example in novels, plays or stories; in poetry it will deal with the types of poem, rhyme, rhythm, free verse for example, or in non-fiction with the main literary concerns of the work. The editor may choose to examine any aspect of the book being studied which he or she considers to be important. The paramount aim is to send the student back to the text. Each study aid will include a series of general questions which require detailed knowledge of the set book: the first of these questions will have notes by the editor of what *might* be included in a written answer. A short list of books considered useful as background reading for the student will be provided at the end.

Graham Handley

The author and his work

Bruce Chatwin is the author of four books, to date. His first, *In Patagonia* (published 1977), is an account of a journey he made through the desolate southern extremity of South America. This was followed by *The Viceroy of Ouidah* (1980), a partly fictionalized biography of a Brazilian slave-trader and the barbaric business he conducted in the African kingdom of Dahomey in the nineteenth century. *On the Black Hill* appeared in 1982. His most recent book (1987) is *Songlines*, which reflects Chatwin's fascination with the nomadic cultures of mankind, in this case the aborigines of Australia.

Chatwin's books do not fit neatly into any single category. Although he won his reputation as a 'travel writer' with *In Patagonia*, Chatwin has expressed (in an interview published in the literary magazine *Granta, No 21*) his irritation with this description of himself. *In Patagonia* holds elements of autobiography, history and fiction or 'lies', as the author himself termed them with humorous bluntness. Similarly, *The Viceroy of Ouidah*, despite its basis in historical reality, is presented as 'a work of the imagination'. Chatwin accepts the description of himself as a wanderer – 'all my plans are geared to the idea of the road', he has said (see *Granta* above) – and, just as the nomad will not endure the stability and stagnation of staying in one place for long, so Chatwin as author does not permit his books to remain fixed in some convenient critical category like 'travel', 'novel' or 'history'.

The comments above may not appear to have much to do with *On the Black Hill*. The books is, after all, a *story*, a novel with characters and events which the writer has invented. It is not about wanderers but about people whose lives are passed within the strict confines of a farming community on the Welsh-English border. It does not deal with strange landscapes or cultures; its setting, if unfamiliar and surprising in some details, is one which is broadly known to us. There is nothing obviously 'exotic' about *On the Black Hill*. But a closer consideration indicates some of the links with Chatwin's other work and, more important, gives us a clearer idea of the breadth and variety of the book.

On the Black Hill is above all the story of the twins Lewis and Benjamin Jones, born at the beginning of the twentieth century. The narrative takes them into their eighties and the death of Lewis in an accident. The book travels from the last century to the present day. The twins have their own history – as we all do. Chatwin describes the major events of their lives – the crises, the turning-points, as well as many minor ones. But History, the material that gets recorded in books and on film and television, forces its way into their lives. In the First World War Benjamin is torn from his brother and sent off for training as a conscript. In the Second World War a German prisoner-of-war is assigned to help the brothers on the farm. These are obvious examples of the way in which momentous public events – such as the catastrophic drama of a war – have their impact on private lives, showing the way in which History invades and becomes entangled with individual histories. Lewis and Benjamin Jones lead isolated lives but even they cannot avoid the ripples spreading from the wider world which they have never chosen to visit. By making their births contemporary with the beginning of this century, Chatwin aligns his principal characters with the period that belongs inescapably to all of us – the twentieth century. Among many other things *On the Black Hill* offers a perspective – fragmentary, one-sided, perhaps distorted – of the last eighty years as it has been glimpsed by ordinary, unremarkable human beings. In at least a couple of senses, therefore, the book is a history.

Chatwin treats his characters rather as a biographer might do. That is, he moves chronologically through their lives recounting events of both major and minor significance. He roots this account in a firm foundation of dates and seasons: 'On Boxing Day of 1924', 'during the terrible winter of '47', 'In the spring of '73', and so on. This helps to reinforce our impression that the author is writing about real people, moving through time (and history) and marking their passage in the way that most of us do, with birthdays, family disasters, moments of elation, bouts of very good or bad weather and great upheavals in the world outside. By adopting the biographical, chronological approach Chatwin gives solidity and roundness to his creations. They become, not shapes conjured up in the author's imagination, but characters 'out there' in a world of changing seasons and memorable dates, some of which will be familiar to us. At the same time it should be noted that Chatwin claims the privilege of the novelist to see into and interpret the hearts and minds of some of his characters. He is able to tell us not only what they look like, what they do, when they do it (all the things that a biography will tell us about its subject), but what they think and feel. A biographer will usually be tentative about the thoughts and feelings of his subject. He has to be, because he, like each of us, cannot really know the exact truth about another person's ideas and emotions. They can be judged only from external evidence, not known from within. The novelist, however, invents characters and is entitled to give them whatever thoughts (or clothes, or habits, etc.) he or she wishes. Chatwin gives to Lewis and Benjamin Jones an external reality (appearance, mannerisms), which would be visible to all; he also gives them an inner life (hopes, fears, sorrows) which cannot be known to any observer, at least not in its detail.

On the Black Hill takes us inside the minds and hearts of several of its principal characters – as many novels do. But it also shows, in its amassing of names, dates, places, family histories, another aspect of Chatwin as a writer: the traveller/observer/biographer who looks at other people – in Patagonia, Australia, Wales – with a tolerant curiosity and respect for the way they lead their lives.

Unlike the characters who appear in Chatwin's other work, most of those who figure in *On the Black Hill* are not wanderers. In fact, they lead lives rooted in a single, fairly restricted patch of land. In the interview referred to earlier the author explained why this was so: 'It always irritated me to be called a travel writer. So I decided to write something about people who never went out. That's how *On the Black Hill* came into being.' There are exceptions. Some of the English people in the novel move around; Theo 'the Tent', who figures in the last few chapters, believes 'that all men were meant to be wanderers', and lives in accordance with this belief. But the Welsh, by and large, do not stray far from their own farms and communities. In the first chapter, for example, we are told that the twins, apart from one seaside holiday, had never been further from their birthplace than Hereford; their eighty years are spent within a compass of twenty miles or so. The reasons for this rooted way of life are partly cultural and economic. And, of course, to stay in one place for a lifetime does not preclude an interest in the wider world (we are told that 'these restricted horizons merely inflamed Lewis's passion for geography') nor, as has already been noted, does it mean those staying in one spot remain untouched by what happens elsewhere. But this fixedness does suggest a most important aspect of *On the Black Hill.*

The book is, in large part, concerned with individuals who live on and from the land. The landscape – and the term includes its geography, its crops and plants, its animals, its weather – is not just a backdrop against which the characters of the novel play out their lives; it is intimately bound up with those lives, to the extent that attempts to describe the links between the men and women and their terrain by words such as 'attachment' or 'dependence' really don't do justice to the intense commitment and sense of belonging that many of the characters show towards their homeland. This is not something that they talk about; indeed, they are not much given to discussing their feelings or explaining their ideas. But the identification between the individual and his land is apparent everywhere. It emerges in the loving knowledge of their surroundings displayed by some of the principal figures in the novel – animals and nature, flowers, trees, seasonal changes, are not sentimentalized or romantically worshipped, they are simply and profoundly *known.* When Lewis runs away, after a family upset, he returns two months later, 'drawn irresistibly in the direction of home'. When some tenant-farmers are threatened with eviction so that their land can be sold profitably, a cry rings out in the auction-room: 'Shall I not die in the farm I were born in?'. Chatwin shows via description and action rather than by direct statement, what the land means to those who live on it. In this he is aided by his own extensive knowledge of the area he is writing about and the fine eye and ear he brings to his evocations of the natural world. He offers to an isolated stretch of the Welsh-English border the same sharpness and freshness of perception that he brings to bear on the African state of Dahomey (in *The Viceroy of Ouidah*) or the wastes of Patagonia. In a sense, all his work celebrates the discovery of parts of the world little known to most of us – a Welsh farming community, half a century ago, may be as 'foreign' to us as a township at the tip of South America.

Although, as I have said already, *On the Black Hill* does not have the obviously 'exotic' locations of Chatwin's other books, it does remind us of the strangeness, the individuality and eccentricity of people and places that we might take for granted, because of their geographical or historical closeness. 'Taking things for granted' is often the product of not bothering to look or listen carefully to what is around us. A thoughtful study of *On the Black Hill* might encourage the reader to look more closely at his or her surroundings, to note and appreciate the individuality of the 'world' each of us inhabits.

Chapter commentaries, textual notes, revision questions and assignments

Chapter I

The opening chapter of *On the Black Hill* introduces the twins, Lewis and Benjamin Jones, whose lives make up the backbone of the novel. We are given some idea of their daily routine, an energetic one despite the fact that they are in their eighties. They are extraordinarily close – they can read each other's minds, to the extent that 'they even quarrelled without speaking' – but they differ in appearance and have distinct talents and preferences among the multitude of jobs that need to be done on their farm. Chatwin describes their home and its furnishings with precision, and tells us a little of their parents. In particular, we learn that they are devoted to the memory of their mother.

The book begins in the present, with the twins entering their ninth decade in the 1980s. But everywhere around them are treasured reminders of their shared past, in the shape of furniture, pictures, ornaments, photographs, and above all the farm itself, known as 'The Vision'. Almost every object mentioned in this chapter will be referred to again in the course of the story, so that we grow to appreciate its significance to the twins. They don't, however, live in, or for, the past. Running the farm demands continual activity. Although childless, they pin their hopes for the future on their great-nephew Kevin, to whom the farm will pass in a few months' time. The chapter ends with the words, 'the promise of new things': after a hard life, each of the twins can still look forward with the optimism that is one of the hallmarks of *On the Black Hill*.

Chapter I serves as a kind of springboard from which the story launches itself into the past. Finding out about the past enables the reader to understand how Lewis and Benjamin Jones have weathered and changed, why they are so devoted to each other, why they idolize the memory of their mother. Much of the rest of the novel is given over to filling out, shading, colouring the sketch provided by the beginning. For this reason it is worth re-reading the opening after you have finished the novel, because there is an accumulation of detail and observation in the first few pages which can only be properly appreciated after you have discovered more about the characters' lives.

Holman Hunt's 'Light of the World' Hunt was a Victorian painter, and 'The Light of the World', often reproduced, is his best-known picture. In it, Christ is depicted as holding a lantern, his other hand raised to knock at a closed door, symbolizing the human heart.
They listened . . . they shaved . . . they tapped the barometer Sometimes the twins scarcely seem to be separate individuals. Chatwin emphasizes that the two often act as one, particularly in routine tasks.
Caractacus Famous British king in West during Roman occupation.
Alice Morgan saw the Virgin hovering over a patch of rhubarb The incongruous positioning of the vision, over the rhubarb patch, perhaps indicates that we are not meant to take the story too seriously.
border of Radnor and Hereford The Welsh county of Radnor no longer exists; the area is part of the larger unit, Powys. The important point here is the siting of the farm exactly astride the Welsh-English border. Opposite windows look out on different countries. This 'doubleness' applies, too, to the farm's occupants: they are twins, of mixed parentage (their mother was English). They, like the farm, can claim to have a foot in either camp, Welsh and English.
He [Benjamin] **did all the cooking, the darning and the ironing** Although the twins share many tasks, the household jobs which would have been the preserve of their mother (including the keeping of accounts) fall to Benjamin – or he finds within himself a special talent for doing them.
Miss Fifield the Tump i.e. Miss Fifield who lives at the Tump (a farm).
Staffordshire A kind of porcelain.
Pool of Bethesda Place in Jerusalem where Jesus performed a miraculous cure. (John, 5.2).
Old Master Term applied to any famous painting (or painter) from before the nineteenth century.
President Carter's failure to rescue the Teheran hostages From 1979–81 American staff were held hostage inside their own embassy in the Iranian capital, Teheran. Jimmy Carter (US President 1976–80) launched a military attempt to rescue them, which failed. The hostages were eventually released when Ronald Reagan became President. This reference to a fairly recent event helps to 'place' the beginning of *On the Black Hill* firmly in the present. Lewis's knowledge of geography is better than his understanding of politics, when he says, of Carter's rescue attempt, 'Him should'a gone to get 'em through Odessa' – Odessa, a Russian port on the Black Sea, would hardly welcome an American military expedition!
the two great colonial empires The empires, coloured pink and mauve in Lewis's old atlas, are respectively Britain and France.
Westward, westward, Hiawatha . . . The lines are from the poem *Hiawatha* by the American poet Longfellow (1807–82). The image of

journeying which they provide hints at the romantic streak in Lewis's temperament.

leg-o'-mutton sleeves Describing the shape of sleeves that are tight at the wrists and fuller further up the arms.

[time's] **healing circle** The twins look forward to transferring ownership of 'The Vision' to their nephew. This family continuity consoles them for their childlessness, and as they trace similarities between a photograph of their mother when young and Kevin's appearance, they can feel content that what was passed to them will be safely passed to another family representative. The 'circle' of time is an image of completion or fulfilment.

Chapter II

Having established something of the Jones twins' characters and circumstances in the present, Chatwin goes back eighty years and more to describe their father, Amos Jones. In the same way a biographer will go back at least a generation or two to show the kind of people and families his subject has sprung from.

Amos is his mother's favourite. Her other children have died or deserted her. In his late twenties he talks of emigrating to Argentina (there were several Welsh colonies there), and the mother hurriedly arranges a marriage to prevent his going away. It is a bleak, unhappy union – Rachel Jones dies, almost by an act of will, after the death of her first baby. Amos's second marriage, to Mary Latimer, is an absolute contrast in almost every respect.

The author suggests the hardship and poverty of the Welsh labourer's life a century ago. For a travelling farm-worker like Amos only the most meagre food and lodging were provided. Nor was there much emotional consolation. Amos's mother, Hannah, tolerated her husband's 'absences and infidelities' in their earlier days together, but the disasters that overtook her children have made her hard and bitter. Amos himself treats his first wife harshly ('She never cried when he hit her'), there is no communication between the two, and the only effect of her death is to turn him into a regular churchgoer. That the marriage is unsuccessful is perhaps not surprising. It is arranged by Hannah Jones more as a means of preventing her son from emigrating than anything else; Amos is not consulted over what is essentially a business negotiation (an unproductive patch of land comes as a dowry with his unwanted wife). Notice here the importance of the wife in the management of household affairs: it is Hannah who keeps off the bailiffs from the little cottage where she lives 'cooped up' with her husband, Hannah who arranges the terms of her son's marriage. Amos's second wife, Mary, will have a similarly dominant role.

Sam the Waggon Example of the Welsh habit of signifying people by their job or something associated with them.

bailiffs Agents of a landlord. The Joneses, like many farm-workers and labourers, would live in rented property under the constant threat of eviction if they failed to maintain payments. That Hannah manages to fend the bailiffs off is a tribute to her toughness and financial shrewdness.

consumption Tuberculosis, the scourge of the ninteenth and early twentieth centuries.

another married a Catholic To marry into another religious denomination was to escape from the narrow confines of Welsh Chapel life, but it was also to cut oneself off from one's roots. For Hannah Jones, this 'defection' of a daughter seems to be a catastrophe equivalent to the deaths of others of her children.

waiting for a farmer to hire him Amos Jones, like other farm-workers, attends the hiring-fairs, hoping to be given a job; without his own land, he has no security or continuity of employment.

He ran away three times This, and other details, suggest a spirit of resistance in Amos – he hopes for something better than the restricted life he is leading.

she sent him away to nurse If a mother was unable to provide her newborn child with her own milk, it was customary to send it to a 'wet-nurse', who would suckle it for a fee.

Chapter III

There is an obvious contrast between the circumstances surrounding Amos's first marriage and the events leading up to his second. The first was a matter of business – a bad business, as it turned out – arranged by Amos's mother. But when Amos first sees Mary Latimer, during a church service conducted by her father, the effect each has on the other is mutual and immediate. Both are held back, however, by awkwardness: Amos is tongue-tied, and Mary has to contend with grief for her dead father and his repressive memory. The Reverend Latimer had once shut his daughter up, to live on a bread and water diet, because of her (entirely innocent) relationship with a man in India. 'The flash of recognition' that passes between Amos and Mary in church is followed by a period in which desperation is mixed with happiness. Neither can easily speak to the other; each gains emotional release by shouting or crying of love – alone. The very strength of their feelings makes them inarticulate. A divide which is not of their making also contributes to their difficulties: differences of class, background and culture. He is the Welsh son of a drover; she is the English daughter of an Old Testament scholar and ex-missionary. These differences become a source of resentment between the couple later in the novel.

She brushed against Amos Jones's shoulder, and she stopped The physical attraction each holds for the other is apparent from the first.
Elijah and his raven In the Old Testament story Elijah was fed by ravens.
Minerva Roman goddess of wisdom.
Eurasian Of mixed perentage, European and Asian.
Platonic love i.e. non-sexual love.

Chapter IV

The uneasy courtship between Amos and Mary reaches a kind of climax in this chapter. Learning that she is about to leave her father's rectory for good – after a summer in which he has been unable to rid himself of the thought of her – Amos rushes back and speaks to her with an authority and confidence that he could not command before. He tells her to sell her father's books (rather than give them away), he consoles her when she accidentally steps on a nestful of lark's eggs, finally he takes her to see the farm which he plans to rent for both of them. Now Mary responds to his decisiveness; later she asserts her own will in the marriage.

The chapter moves from Mary's world to the one that Amos inhabits – appropriately so, since he is leading her from her father's house to the one that they will share together. As they ride towards the Black Hill to inspect 'The Vision', they move on to *his* territory. He knows the people who live there, and their secrets, just as they know him.

By now, you should be starting to note some of the features of Chatwin's style: the short, darting paragraphs, which give to the book a sense of immediacy and nervous vitality; the selection of detail which is colourful, odd or dramatic; the mingling of narrative with description of landscape and nature.

drabbet Coarse linen.
having to go into service i.e. having to go to work as a household servant, an unattractive possibility for an educated and middle-class woman like Mary.
her father's shade Her father's ghost or spirit.
Her straw hat was crowned with roses . . . Both have dressed up, or bought something new, sensing the importance of the occasion.

Chapter V

Amos Jones and Mary Latimer face considerable opposition to their marriage plans. Mary, in particular, must confront the hostility of some of the Welsh and the suspicion of most of the English. Mrs Bickerton, whose family owns 'The Vision', gently attempts to undermine Mary's resolve; the agent who deals with the Bickertons' property is obstructive; even Mary's sister writes to tell her that she is marrying beneath her. There is clearly a difference of class between prospective husband and wife, and bound up with this is the distinction between Welsh and English. Roughly speaking, it is the distinction between tenant and landlord, worker and employer, private soldier and officer. As the book continues, the resentment of the Welsh for the 'dirty Saxons' who intrude into so much of their lives comes to seem increasingly justified.

Mary uses her English background and connections to get what she – and Amos – want: immediate tenancy of the farm. But this cultural or class 'advantage' is double-edged and the source of later bitterness for herself and her husband. That the couple tread down obstacles to reach their wedding-day (in August 1899 – see Chapter II) is a testimony to their love, and their determination. The broken-down state of the farm stirs their imagination; the moment when Amos makes what is not so much a proposal as a proposition – 'Could you live in this?' – is accompanied by the traditional props of romantic love, moonlight and a nightingale which 'flung liquid notes into the darkness'. There is no doubt of the intensity of their commitment to each other after this.

the West India trade The trade was in sugar – and in slaves to produce the crop.
'four months gone' Pregnant (and therefore forced to marry).
'China or Indian?' i.e. tea.

the post of governess Mrs Bickerton attempts to 'rescue' Mary from marriage by offering her a job in her family.
milch Milk-producing.
the piano and four-poster Both these valuable pieces of furniture have been mentioned in earlier chapters; gradually, Chatwin shows us why such things are important possessions. They are a link with people and places in the past.

Questions and assignments on Chapters I-V

1 In your own words describe the differences (of appearance, behaviour, talents) between the twins from the evidence of Chapter I.

2 What do we learn about the relationship between the Welsh and the English in these opening chapters?

Assignments

1 Mary Latimer gets a letter from her sister before her wedding (Chapter V). She destroys it. Put yourself in her position, and write the reply she might have made to her sister's objections to the marriage.

2 Most of the pieces of furniture, pictures, ornaments, etc. in 'The Vision' have a value for the Jones twins which is unconnected with money. Write about something in your own possession, or your family's, which has a similar significance. Explain how and why it became important.

3 From the information given in these chapters, draw up a family tree for the Jones twins.

Chapter VI

The early days of the marriage are not easy. After eight months Mary feels that 'she had sat for years . . . in the same trap, living with the same bad-tempered man'. She tries to improve and refine her environment, to import the middle-class habits of her father's rectory into the roughcast walls of a working farm. Amos's response is to feel constrained and irritable. He loses his temper, gets drunk. There is open hostility between Mary and her mother-in-law. She can't do anything right: when she talks quite naturally with her neighbours about animals or crops, Amos is merely made very uncomfortable. They have their 'honeymoon' period, hard-working though it is, and there is evidently a strong physical bond between the two, but the differences (of background, culture and expectations) seem so strong that the future of the marriage is thrown into doubt.

the Passion Term used to describe Christ's torments on the cross. Mary finds it hard to concentrate on worship with her husband beside her at communion; physical passion replaces the religious one.

Chapel-folk One of the most significant divisions in the novel is between 'Church' and 'Chapel'. The term 'chapel' embraces the various denominations (Baptists, Congregationalists, Methodists) which are separate from the Church of England. Mary's father was a rector in the latter, and it was in church (rather than chapel) that the couple first met. Later Mary deserts her 'mother' church and becomes one of the 'chapel-folk' because she feels more comfortable there (see Chapter XVII). 'Chapel' would be considered a more purely *Welsh* institution than the Church of England, and to attend chapel would mark one as more firmly embedded in Welsh tradition and culture.

Border Barons The overlords, created by William I and other English monarchs, who occupied territories on the Anglo-Welsh border. They provided a buffer between the two countries.

scab . . . colic . . . laminitis Mary isn't putting on an act when she talks about these animal diseases. Her talk shows how familiar farm life has become to her. Ironically, Amos is irritated by her knowledge of his world.

Burning Ghats In India, places beside a river where bodies are cremated.

Yet – as Amos never tired of reminding them – her feet had trodden in the steps of His Feet Although resentful of many of the changes which his wife tries to introduce into his life, Amos is proud of one thing which underlines how different Mary's past has been from his own: she has toured the Holy Land with her father, and entrances her Welsh guests with first-hand descriptions of the landscape.

Rose of Sharon Mentioned in the Old Testament (Sharon was the name of a plain), like the four names that follow in the same paragraph.

Ruth . . .; Jacob and Esau; Joseph . . .; . . . Hagar Figures who feature in famous Old Testament stories. Ruth, an inhabitant of Moab, went to Bethlehem after the death of her husband, with her mother-in-law. Gleaning corn in the land where she had made her voluntary exile, she met Boaz, who became her second husband. The story of the brothers, Jacob and Esau, and the trickery used by the former to get his father's blessing, is well known. Joseph's 'patchwork coat' was given him by his father; the same coat of many colours was dipped in goat's blood by

Joseph's jealous brothers as evidence to offer to their father that he was dead. Hagar was a servant-girl who bore Abraham a son and was later rejected. These three stories are in Genesis; the first can be found in the Book of Ruth. Their attraction for the Welsh farmers is that they are good tales which happen to have a vague connection with farming activities.

Mrs Beeton's Book of Household Management A famous guide to cookery and running a household, first published in the mid-nineteenth century but popular well into the twentieth. As the context of the reference suggests, the ambitious menus of Mrs Beeton are not appropriate for the Joneses' way of life.

Chapter VII

The chapter builds to the climax of the twins' birth, an event which is followed, within a few days, by the death of Hannah Jones, Amos's mother. If the author is making the point that birth and death exist side by side, then it is not one that he labours over. Hannah Jones's departure does not appear to be regretted by anyone – least of all herself – and there is grim comedy in the way she plants herself in her daughter-in-law's household and very slowly knits the pair of long white socks that will cover her dead feet when she is 'laid out'. Still just alive, she has nothing left to express except a relish for the morbid. Her husband, on the other hand, is rejuvenated by contact with his daughter-in-law. Sam the Waggon grows flirtatious in Mary's company; they play duets (he 'still owned an ancient fiddle'), even dance the polka. Despite the death with which the chapter concludes, its mood is much sunnier than that of the previous one. Amos looks forward to the birth of a boy with proud anxiety; Mary recovers her love for her husband.

Relief of Mafeking Mafeking, a town in South Africa, was besieged during the Boer War. When the siege was lifted after eight months by the coming of British forces, (on May 17th, 1900) the occasion was one of great national rejoicing. Colonel Baden-Powell, later the founder of the Boy Scouts, was commander of the garrison during the siege. This historical reference, one of many in *On the Black Hill*, helps to anchor the characters' lives in a particular period. The public jubilation of the Relief of Mafeking also ushers in a more relaxed period in relations between Mary and Amos: relief after the gloom of winter.

layette Baby-clothes. Amos regards the outfit as too 'pretty' for the boy he expects.

'Mother belongs here. She must stay.' Not for the first time Amos is a victim of divided loyalties, and comes down on his mother's side. Hannah Jones sees it as her duty to attend the last weeks of her daughter-in-law's pregnancy (although her presence unnerves Mary).

Chapter VIII

The narrative now centres on the twins. Less is seen through adult eyes, more is glimpsed through the children's stranger vision. The individuality – or oddness – of a child's view of the world is accentuated here because Lewis and Benjamin are both individuals, but neither seems to have a sense of individual identity. Temperamentally they are distinct: Lewis is strong and fearless where Benjamin is anxious and cowardly. But their first memory is of an event where their temperamental, even their physical separateness seems to blur. Benjamin is stung by a wasp but it is Lewis who feels the pain; he has the 'power to draw the pain from his brother, and take it on himself'. When the twins have grown a little they refuse every adult attempt to differentiate between them. To be different is to be separate, and then perhaps separated. They won't accept Sunday suits in different colours; they run from a bossy woman who has found a distinguishing mole behind Benjamin's ear. In all their activities they deny that they are two people. To make themselves still more impenetrable to the outside world they even use a private language.

Amos and Mary separately enlist the children in activities that reflect their priorities: Mary gets them to help with the housework, Amos is determined to introduce them to farm-life, and is impatient with the 'book-learning' his wife is introducing to the twins.

truckle bed Low bed on castors that can be pushed under another.
'God's spitting' The twins' description of snow, which they have never seen before, conveys the odd, near-poetic quality of a young child's outlook. Notice that Lewis and Benjamin speak in unison.
Lewis answered Benjamin and Benjamin answered Lewis To be given a name – and to answer to it – is to be distinguished from others; the twins instinctively desire to remain one, and not to be picked out as separate individuals. They frustrate the grown-up world's need to tell them apart by confusing their names.
They saw an angry pink creature biting Mary's breast Horror and jealousy are the twins' first reactions to their baby sister – to them, she seems barely human. Notice how the birth of Mary's third child earns only a few lines and is glimpsed entirely through the eyes of Lewis and Benjamin, indications of where the focus of the novel now lies.

Chapter IX

What is perhaps the twins' first experience of the harshness, even brutality, of farm-life comes when their father kills the runt (i.e. the smallest, weakest pig in a litter) even though the boys have adopted it as a pet. We already know that Amos is determined that his children should not be 'mollycoddled', and it is probable that he kills the pig to jolt them out of what he would see as a sentimental attitude towards animals. He will make men, and farmers, out of them. They think of him as a murderer, and shy away from him. Their hatred increases when they see him fussing over their baby sister.

Old Sam had . . . slipped into second childhood The twins and Sam have more in common than any of them has with Amos. Sam takes on some child-like qualities in his old age.

Questions and assignments on Chapters VI-IX

1 Within a few months of her marriage Mary is evidently wondering whether she has done the wrong thing. Taking evidence from the text (particularly Chapter VI) explain her point of view.

2 What examples does the narrative give us of the twins' acting as one, rather than as separate individuals in the first years of their lives? Can you find other examples of twins in literature?

Assignments

1 Using the twins' first memory (Chapter VIII) as an example, write about the earliest things you can remember and try to explain why these have remained in your mind.

2 The twins are very close to Sam, their grandfather. Write about a member of your family with whom you feel a particular closeness.

Chapter X

With their grandfather the twins go on walks, one (the 'Welsh' one) in the direction of the Black Hill, the other (the 'English' one) to Lurkenhope Park, where the Bickertons live. The walks thus suggest the twins' divided parentage. On the English walk they befriend the head-gardener at Lurkenhope and achieve a near-magical vision of a girl and man boating on the castle lake. This is the world that their mother is entitled to enter, even if she is not truly at home in it. On the Welsh walk they travel into more barren territory, and the twins are introduced to the occupants of the Watkins homestead. This is the land of their father. It would be incorrect, however, to jump to the conclusion that the 'English' side represents the wealth and privilege which will always be denied the likes of the Joneses, while the 'Welsh' side offers only friendship in deprivation. The two worlds, English and Welsh, are not rigidly distinct; there is a border (which is said to run through the middle of 'The Vision') but there is no real barrier; the two 'sides' mingle, penetrate each other. The closeness, the inter-dependency and the frequent hostility of Anglo-Welsh relations echo something of the complex ties that bind the twins together.

At the end of this chapter, it is the hostility between the two nations which we note. On their Black Hill walk Lewis, outraged at discovering trespassers on their 'territory', hits out at Reggie Bickerton, who is taking photographs of two friends. Reggie captures and spanks Lewis. Mary is ashamed of her children's behaviour, because they have unthinkingly shown their attitude towards the 'dirty Saxons' with whom their mother still has much in common. At the same time she is 'ashamed of being ashamed of them': family loyalties tug her in one direction, class and nationality in another.

Golgotha Calvary, the place of crucifixion for Jesus and the two thieves.

Benjamin burst into tears Lewis's fantasy that he will marry Miss Bickerton one day suggests to Benjamin that he will be parted from his brother.

Church-folk As opposed to chapel-folk (see note on Chapter VI).

menhir Large standing stone, marking some significant site. Sam's explanations of what this particular stone signifies show confused memories of superstitious tradition.

Prince Llewellyn . . . the Black Vaughan Llewellyn is supposed to have killed one of his dogs in error, believing that the animal had killed the child which it had been left to guard. According to the folk-tale the dog had in fact protected the baby against a marauding wolf. The Black Vaughan was a well-known Herefordshire ghost!

Chapter XI

Mary's friendship with the Reverend Thomas Tuke is prompted partly by her sense of isolation. Talking to him is an escape from the farm-life which, she confesses to the vicar alone, depresses her. She has nobody to meet her on the same intellectual level. She must also be drawn by the similarities between him and her father: he too is a scholar, and is something of an 'exile' in this landscape; like Mary, he has travelled; there is even a physical resemblance ('A tall, bony man with a mass of snowy curls') – another reminder for her. The Reverend Tuke lends her books, shows off his rare flowers, and, more importantly, takes over the question of the twins' education. By herself, Mary would probably not be able to overcome Amos's hostility to education, a hostility that springs from his fear that the boys might be raised above their 'station' in life and no longer want to remain on the farm. The vicar uses the authority of his position and a naturally commanding manner to impress an unwelcome truth on Amos: 'Bright boys, both of them! High time they were in school!'

Homer Greek epic poet, probable author of the *Iliad* and *Odyssey*.
hexameters Greek and Latin verse measures.
a Cambridge rowing blue i.e. he had represented the university in rowing. A slightly odd mixture of qualities in the Reverend Tuke – a huntsman who collects rare plants, a scholar who is more interested in the classics than the Bible – make him 'a mystery' to the parishioners. He is a little out of place, like Mary Jones.
Euripides Greek author of tragedies (in fifth century BC).
Upanishads Ancient philosophical works from India.
Zola One of the most famous and outspoken of nineteenth-century French novelists. The range of books which the clergyman lends to Mary shows the extent of his literary interests – and her desire to learn.
'Yokels!' she said, bitterly Compare this incident with Mary's attempt to write a letter to Mrs Bickerton apologizing for her sons' behaviour (end of previous chapter).
He would have liked to work, but it was the Sabbath Amos has an instinctive respect for his religion, the church and its ministers. He is a pious man (and observes the commandment forbidding work on Sunday). Although he curses the vicar for his interference, his children still begin their formal education.

Chapter XII

In the middle of this chapter a group photograph is described: the Jones family, together with Jim Watkins from the Rock, come to work at the hay-making in 1909. The chapter as a whole is a kind of photo album, brief portraits of the twins at various stages of their development. So we see them at school, and unjustly punished for 'cheating'; then at play, children's games, fighting. What is stressed throughout is the twins' intimacy. The only threat to this comes from an early, mild piece of sexual experimenting between Lewis and Rosie Fifield. Even as he sets off in pursuit of this 'impish girl of ten', however, 'Benjamin's plaintive wailing reined him back'. Lewis is always mindful of his weaker brother. Benjamin's summons is stronger than any other call.

Both . . . swore to be enemies for ever Even when placed on opposite sides, in a football match or a child's game, Lewis and Benjamin are unable to act apart for more than a few moments. Their absolute loyalty to each other takes precedence over everything else.

Chapter XIII

'Jim the Rock' comes to work at The Vision. He takes the Jones twins on a rabbit hunt, using his pet ferret. Caught in a bad hailstorm, Benjamin develops pneumonia and comes near to death. He recovers, but 'not without a change in his personality'. The illness is important not merely because it is one of the landmarks of his childhood but because it seems to give his nature some shape or twist that he will bear for the rest of his life. In particular, his dependency on Lewis is accentuated: now he walks, not beside Lewis, but literally in his brother's footsteps, breathing 'the air that he had breathed'. In the first chapter of *On the Black Hill* Chatwin suggests that it is Benjamin who plays the traditional 'feminine' role in the household in old age (he does the cooking, darning, etc.). The beginnings of this can be seen here when Benjamin bakes a cake for Lewis's tea and then, like a devoted housewife, breathlessly waits for his brother's verdict on his cooking. A cruder example of the feminine aspect of his nature is shown by his dressing up in his mother's clothes, something that horrifies Mary – not so much for its own sake as because Amos might discover him. This is not to say that

Benjamin is presented as an effeminate character. It is rather that the twins are completely complementary in their lives: the more 'masculine' streak in Lewis is answered by its counterpart of a 'feminine' side in Benjamin.

In a different way, it is Lewis who follows his brother. Benjamin's illness gives Mary the opportunity to pass on to him some of her 'book' learning. This provokes Lewis's jealous attempt to copy him, to become a 'scholar' too. From this point in their lives, and as a result of a minor incident, it is the bookish boy who takes control of their pocket-money; seventy years later, we learn, it is still he who manages the household accounts. Patterns established in childhood persist into age. Lewis's life-long fascination with aviation – more specifically, with aircraft crashes – also has its roots at this period of his development. A fact learnt at school, a newspaper report of a disaster at an air-display, spark this faintly morbid concern.

Chatwin conveys effectively the way in which interests, habits, skills acquired at an early age shape our later lives. Each twin starts to mark out a territory of his own, demonstrates different strengths and weaknesses.

Bleriot The first man to fly across the English Channel (1909). Lewis's interest in aviation may spring partly from a desire to have something to match his brother's more intellectual concerns, but it also points towards the romantic aspect of his nature which is excited by the idea of distance and travel.

Questions and assignments on Chapters X-XIII

1 Show how Mary becomes concerned for her sons' education and the steps she takes to do something about it.

2 It is not only through formal schooling that the twins are educated. Describe and discuss some of the other experiences that contribute to their growing-up process in these chapters.

3 What different qualities and habits begin to emerge in Lewis and Benjamin at this stage? How far are these opposed, or complementary?

Assignments

1 Describe an interest of your own, which may have started from something minor, or an experience which you consider has 'shaped' your life.

Chapter XIV

Mary's friendship with the Reverend Tuke, and his concern for the boys' well-being, prompts the clergyman to offer to take them with him on his yearly sketching holiday at his sister's home in south-west Wales. It is the furthest the Jones twins will ever travel. This fact, which we are told in the first chapter of the novel, gives poignancy to Lewis's dream of becoming a sailor. Listening to an old sailor's tales of rounding Cape Horn, gazing out to the horizon and imagining himself 'on the crow's-nest of a full-rigged ship', the more adventurous of the twins is romantically caught by exotic ambition.

The seaside is a new world to Lewis and Benjamin. The middle-class, 'artistic' household of the two English women, Miss Catharine Tuke and her 'sorrowful' companion, is also something they have never experienced before, and at first they feel uncomfortable there. But the excitement of exploration and discovery soon overcomes their unease.

'I know your kind. All fancy talk and holidays by the seaside!' Amos's suspicion of his wife's plans for their children brings to the surface his lurking anxieties that the twins are being brought up in a way that will make them unfit for farm-life. He can't forget that his background and Mary's are at odds ('your kind'), nor escape from the prejudiced belief that all her attempts at education amount to nothing more than 'fancy talk'. In this case Mary has a strong argument on her side: the holiday is necessary for Benjamin's health.

He had taken a swipe at the porter The latent hostility between the two nations, Welsh and English, can spill over into violence, as in this incident at the station.

The canvas . . . showed a beautiful young man . . . pierced through and through with arrows A picture of St Sebastian, one of the early Christian martyrs, put to death with arrows. In the previous chapter we are told how Benjamin became preoccupied with death, after recovering from his illness.

He had seen the Giant Patagonians . . . Patagonia is a vast area at the tip of South America, fertile land for legends and travellers' tales. It was the subject of Bruce Chatwin's first book.

their scarlet gills reminded the boys of the carnations in Mr Earnshaw's green-house A good example of one of the ways in which a novelist can build up the impression of a self-contained 'world' in a piece of fiction. A minor detail, a striking colour, brings to mind a parallel. Just as the twins are reminded of one colour by another, so the reader should be reminded on an earlier detail in their lives (their friendship with the gardener, Mr Earnshaw – see chapter X) by the reference here. As more happens, there is more to remember. By accumulating detail and impression in layer on layer, the writer can create the image of an increasingly dense and complex world.

Chapter XV

After chronicling the twins' early years, with their excitements and disappointments, the narrative enters a darker phase. A violent and protracted feud breaks out between the Jones and Watkins families. It brings premature age to Amos and Mary, causes the near-collapse of their marriage, and results in the wanton destruction of stock and property. The Joneses largely escape the consequences of the First World War (although Benjamin is conscripted in the final months), and it is ironic that they should suffer – and, in the case of Amos, bring about – the effects of a small-scale 'war' with their neighbours. Indeed, the feud, in its pointlessness and viciousness, foreshadows on a minute scale the catastrophe that was to overtake Europe in 1914. But the beginnings of the Jones-Watkins war, as dramatized in this chapter, are small. Sheep stray from one man's land to another's, there is a dispute over boundaries, petty theft provokes retaliation. Here Amos is seen to have right on his side; he runs a well-conducted farm. The Watkins, by contrast are slovenly and dishonest.

The integrity of the Estate had been called into question The Vision is part of the Lurkenhope Estate; any tampering with the farm's boundaries is therefore an attack, indirectly, on the English landlords. Notice that Amos isn't easily provoked, but keeps his temper in the encounters with Watkins and makes use of the law and authority. He resorts to violence only when another theft occurs at the farm.

Chapter XVI

The events described in the next two chapters mark a low-point in Amos and Mary's marriage. The feud with the Watkins reaches a more violent pitch, and Amos's fury boils over on to his own family. He is vicious and mean-spirited towards his wife and the twins; he hobbles them with his own misery and rage, beating the boys for 'speaking in a classy accent', hitting Mary 'for putting a second pinch of tea in the pot'. Nothing goes right for her: on a peace-making visit to the Rock, she is set upon by the Watkins' dog; the Reverend Tuke dies; so too does 'her other friend', Sam the Waggon, Amos's father. Her husband's mood does not improve with a change in the seasons.

Like several other sections of *On the Black Hill* this chapter exhibits the underside of rural life, and shows that violence and stupidity can flourish there as anywhere else. Chatwin describes all this, unsentimentally, without direct condemnation of any of the characters involved. Indeed, we see that Amos himself is as much a figure to be pitied as to be criticized. Implicit in the narrative, however, is admiration for Mary Jones: the mainstay of the family, waiting desperately for the return of her husband's love, and in the meantime suffering under his words and blows without attempting retaliation.

INRI The initial letters of the Latin inscription above the cross and reading in translation, 'Jesus of Nazareth King of the Jews'.
'He was a heathen' See Amos's earlier comment on the Reverend Tuke in Chapter XI. He doesn't attempt to sympathize with Mary.
flames i.e. loves, girl-friends.
How tall they'd grown! The paragraph beginning here reminds us of Mary's concern for her children as well as of the fact that they are growing up.

Chapter XVII

As the feud gets worse, Amos becomes more frantic and irrational. He looks to the Bible for support and he finds an ally in the new Congregational minister; for this reason he abandons the Church of England. Mary follows, at first only to humour her unpredictable husband, but eventually she discovers a greater comfort and fulfilment in 'chapel' than she ever had in her father's church. This shift of loyalty is perhaps a sign of her gradual growth towards the land and the way of life that she embraced when she married Amos. Her allegiance to him undergoes increasingly severe strain until the moment when her fear and patience both vanish, after he has struck her once too often. From that moment the balance of power in the household changes. A letter written to her sister in Cheltenham panics Amos, who grows suddenly submissive at the prospect of her leaving. As he grows more subdued, Mary's love flourishes again – appropriately, it is spring, the time when in previous years the couple have patched up their relationship.

Greek cross Cross having arms of the same length.
doctrine of Transubstantiation (Catholic) doctrine that the bread and wine, consecrated and shared out during mass, are converted in their inner essence to the body and blood of Christ, although retaining the outward appearance of bread and wine. The new Minister would not be able to grasp such doctrinal subtleties, Mary thinks – he is a long way from the scholarship of her father or the Reverend Tuke.
'The sin of Jezebel' Jezebel 'painted her face' and dressed herself up, according to the Old Testament (2 Kings, ix), so becoming a by-word for female shamelessness and vanity.
He . . . took the twins away from school So that they could work full-time on the farm. This seems to be an act of spite; he is crushing all Mary's hopes for her sons' education.
Commonwealth Period in English history (1649–60) covering the Protectorate of Oliver Cromwell, and a time of growth of the number of Noncomformists in Wales.
the Upper Room Place of the Last Supper.
fakirs and flagellants Religious men who deliberately endure hardship or suffering as a means of self-discipline. The comparison suggests that Amos's fanaticism over the Watkins feud has become confused with his new-found loyalty to 'chapel'. His suffering has acquired religious overtones.
Book of Job Old Testament story of the man overtaken by a string of disasters and, in his endurance of them, an image of patience. Amos obviously identifies himself with this figure.
Wuthering Heights Emily Bronte's famous novel (1847).
'I'm not even going to tell you what's in it.' Mary's sister's letter is cold and dismissive but, ironically, the mere fact of letters being exchanged has been enough to make Amos feel some guilt about his treatment of Mary. By the time she gets the reply, her love has flared again, like the fire described in the final sentence of the chapter.

Questions and assignments on Chapters XIV-XVII

1 Why does Mary strike up a friendship with the Reverend Tuke? What do you think each person gains from the other?

2 Describe the stages that lead to the outbreak of 'war' between the Jones and Watkins families.

Assignments

1 Write a dialogue between Benjamin and Lewis commenting on their father's decision to remove them from school and put them to work on the farm. Remember that their responses are likely to be different.

2 Write part or all of the letter that Mary sends to her sister, explaining why she must now leave her husband. Alternatively, write the entries which Mary might include in a diary, if she were to keep one, for some part of this period.

Chapter XVIII

Once again the narrative centres on the twins, as they move into adolescence. Growing up also means, to an extent, growing apart. Their mother feels that at some time in the future they will 'slide back into the old, familiar pattern of dependence'. For the present, however, the emphasis is on the differences between Lewis and Benjamin. It is the latter who follows the more unusual path. While his brother flirts with the local girls, Benjamin falls into religious day-dreaming. Adolescent moodiness turns his Welsh landscape into a holy land; Benjamin's paradise is found in The Vision. It's worth noting that Chatwin treats Benjamin's insights seriously: they are not laughed at or condescended to, or treated as the unhealthy manifestations of a suppressed sexual instinct which, in Lewis, finds a more natural outlet. Chatwin simply reports how Benjamin invests his surroundings – home, hills, animals – with a mystical, religious significance. And since much of the novel is devoted to tracing out the links between people and their land, we should by now be able to appreciate something of Benjamin's sense of the holy particularity of the place where he lives. The account is not without humour, though. In the picture, 'The Broad and Narrow Path', which Benjamin studies so eagerly, the right-hand side showing the way up to heaven is 'unmistakably' Welsh in its detail, even reminding Benjamin of the brochure for a local resort. Wales and Heaven are synonymous!

Benjamin is unusual in the intensity of his religious day-dreaming but he is like many young people in being very conservative. He likes things exactly as they are, wants to remain with Lewis forever and do precisely what his much-admired brother does. While Lewis's dreams are the traditional boyish ones of travel and aircraft, Benjamin's ideal is to stay still. Here again the twins complement each other.

Count Zeppelin German inventor (1838–1917) of the airship widely used during the First World War.

'The Way of Perdition' i.e. the route to Hell. The statues on either side of the gateway in the picture represent physical love (Venus) and drunkenness (Bacchus is the god of wine). The kind of behaviour disapproved of by the strict non-comformist – gambling, travelling by train on Sunday – leads, somewhat implausibly, to the real sins of theft and murder which are depicted on the road to Hell in the religious print.

Chapter XIX

The First World War, a black thread running through the next four chapters, makes no immediate impact on the Joneses. They attend a lecture, in fact a recruiting meeting, at which Mary is afraid Amos intends to make a protest against the war. But he says nothing, and any objections to the fighting are overwhelmed by a surge of patriotic feeling, fuelled by a ranting vicar, who gives to the war the moral respectability of a crusade against a 'devilish' enemy. The Joneses' minister, too, claims that they are engaged on 'a Crusade for Christ'. Church and chapel have come together in an unholy alliance to proclaim the rightness and necessity of battle.

The war and its aftermath are seen through Welsh eyes. Appeals to patriotism – 'what England expects of every man' – raise the question, asked but never answered in this chapter, 'What about Wales?' It is during this section of *On the Black Hill* that we have the sharpest sense of the distinction between the two nations, England and Wales. It is a distinction that speaks against the larger and more powerful of the two. English characters, such as Mr Arkwright (see Chapter XX) or Colonel Bickerton, are viewed unsympathetically. The Welsh are seen as exploited victims – at first clamouring eagerly to volunteer and later, as the war takes an increasing toll, being conscripted or exempted by arrogant military tribunals which have, effectively, the power of life and death. The class-system remains: the English landlords and their agents insulated from the worst effects of war by wealth or privilege, the Welsh tenants bearing the brunt. Colonel Bickerton claims that the war will create a new aristocracy (those who did their duty by their country), but the narrative demonstrates the hollowness of that assertion.

her apron was streaked with purple stains Descriptive detail that (like the later colouring of the sky, 'crimson to gunmental') foreshadows bloodshed.
'Besides, it'll probably be over by Christmas.' Mary's comment reflects the almost universal expectation that the war would be quickly done with.
Lord Kitchener Secretary of State for War.
the murder of an Archduke The assassination of the Austrian Archduke Ferdinand on June 28th, 1914 was the event that lead to the outbreak of war.
Mons Site of battle and a well-known British retreat.
Tommies British soldiers (privates).
This was how Jim the Rock went to war The comment indicates that the motives for enlisting were mixed; Jim joins up to get away from home and as a gesture of chivalrous dedication to Miss Isobel Bickerton, in whose seductive presence he hovers 'mouth agape'.

Chapter XX

After more than three years of the war, that was to have finished by Christmas 1914, the twins find themselves liable for military service. An officious English solicitor comes to The Vision to assess the needs of the farm, and decides that there is insufficient land to justify more than one son's remaining to work on it. Arkwright's high-handed attitude rouses Amos to a pitch of defiant – but useless – fury. We have already seen something of his opposition to the war. His pacifism has tangled roots: on the one hand his religious fervour causes him to interpret the destruction as 'God's visitation' on sinners, and the sincerity of his belief makes him question the authenticity of churchmen who gloss over the Biblical commandment forbidding killing; on the other, he is determined that his sons will never fight in what he regards as an 'English' war. As a result of this Amos breaks with his minister and takes the twins to meetings of Conscientious Objectors. National pride, hostility towards the English, genuine principle – all combine to make him an unrelenting opponent of the war.

Amos's attitude gets some endorsement from the author. Even Mary, who in the beginning had been a believer in Victory, comes to think that her husband may be correct as the news of one bloody catastrophe after another strikes home. The vicious treatment given to the conscientious objectors is touched on, and their lonely stand (and support for the ideal of universal brotherhood) is perceived as admirable, even if incapable of bringing about change. The one beneficial effect of the war is to bring a truce, ironically, to the Jones-Watkins feud.

Cities of the Plain The cities of Sodom and Gomorrah, destroyed with fire and brimstone because of their wickedness, according to the story in Genesis. Amos interprets the war as divine retribution (on the morally lax English).
Nebuchadnezzar King of Babylon who took Jerusalem, and carried off Jews into captivity in his kingdom.
Rechabites In the Old Testament a sect that abstained from drink and was commanded not to live in houses. The Rechabites whose meetings Amos attends are strict abstainers and pacifists.
Sixth Commandment Thou shalt not kill.
Conscientious Objectors Those who object, on moral grounds, to military service. As the chapter indicates, such a course could often be dangerous.
Somme Battle (1916) involving very heavy British losses.
Standard Field Service Postcards Impersonal communications introduced during the First World War. The soldier put a mark by the appropriate printed comment. Aggie, who cannot read, interprets Jim's 'cross' as a message of his death.
letter . . . from the King To announce a death.
Passchendaele Battle (1917) which involved great waste of life.
'Them'll die apart . . .' Amos is violently opposed to his sons' conscription, but his remark shows how he now accepts the fact that the twins are indispensable to one another. A few years before he had made efforts to separate them.

Chapter XXI

Amos's words to Mr Arkwright (see last note above) are no exaggeration. When the father sends Lewis off to a neighbouring farm – as a means of evading the military tribunal – Benjamin begins, literally, to pine away. He loses the sense of his own identity: when he looks at his reflection, it is not himself he sees, but Lewis; finally, his shaving mirror gives back no image at all. Without his other 'half' he cannot function. Lewis manages more successfully, even enjoying his time on the other farm. At a distance, however, he still thinks of his brother, and when

Benjamin gets lost in a snow-storm Lewis knows not only that his twin is in danger of dying but also exactly where to find him. Benjamin's near-death is perhaps not an accident. We are told at the beginning of the chapter that he had thoughts of killing himself, after Lewis's departure, and the first, reproachful words he says to his rescuer are, 'You left me'. Here, as elsewhere in the story, Benjamin is shown to have the strength of his weakness, as it were. Lewis will always respond to his appeals for help; he knows intuitively when his brother is in trouble or danger and cannot detach himself from Benjamin's suffering. In a sense, therefore, the less strong of the pair is actually the more powerful, because he knows that a call for help will always bring Lewis to him.

He liked to tinker with the new-fangled machinery The first indication of Lewis's interest in 'modern' farming equipment, the kind of thing unavailable at The Vision.
Saul Oratorio by Handel.
civvies i.e. civilian clothes (rather than military uniform). The remark illustrates the public hostility towards those young men who appeared to have avoided military service.
feeling very low Despite being more worldly and extrovert than his brother, Lewis is still unprepared to deal with the teasing, bad temper and threats that the townspeople casually use towards him. In this section he appears very much as the simple country boy set down in a depressing and unfriendly urban environment.
Clemenceau French Prime Minister in the last stages of the First World War (1914–1918).

Chapter XXII

In this chapter we see the clearest evidence of the way in which Welsh interests are made subordinate to English 'patriotic' requirements. There is no attempt at even-handedness on Chatwin's part. The (English) members of the military tribunal which sends Benjamin off for training are presented as near-caricatures. They come to their meeting in a pious glow; the clergyman on the committee feels 'exhilarated by notions of youth and sacrifice' – but not, of course, of self-sacrifice. They have fed and drunk well. They are pompous, alert to any suggestion of criticism of their task, and always ready to guard their own positions. Colonel Bickerton, we are told, has already exempted from service 'two of his hunt servants, and his valet', so he is the more eager to find suitable candidates to send to the front line. When Benjamin has the courage to ask the vicar whether he believes in the Sixth Commandment, he is accused of 'gross impertinence' and sent for training as punishment, we feel, because he has followed Amos's line in suggesting that there may be a contradiction between the conduct of the war and Biblical teaching. The other cases that come before the Tribunal are treated with a similar briskness and lack of feeling. Here Chatwin affirms the accusations that were expressed in the bitterest terms by some of the writers who had actual experience of the war (such as the poets Wilfred Own and Siegfried Sassoon): that young men were, in effect, condemned by the middle-aged and the old; that the latter, whether as members of tribunals or as military commanders, despatched with indifference a younger generation to slaughter.

The second half of the chapter shows that the Jones family's fears are well justified. Benjamin is curiously calm ('The war's as good as over now'), but his departure provokes a violent response in Mary, who believes that her husband has deliberately 'sacrificed their weaker son', her favourite. Ironically, Amos has struggled to save both, explaining to the treacherous solicitor, Arkwright, that his sons are 'not two persons, but one'. When Benjamin is mistreated, even tortured in Hereford Barracks – and the 'punishments' are the more shocking for being so flatly summarized – it is Lewis who receives his twin's pain but is powerless to alleviate it. Victory brings celebration, but not for the dangerously ill Benjamin. Brief paragraphs describing his plight are set against those that catalogue the public rejoicing at the defeat of the Germans. The victory seems hollow when the human loss and waste that went to make it are measured. Benjamin's sufferings are hardly the worst (real veterans of the fighting are described later) but they are bad enough. The chapters that cover the Great War period are not a dispassionate historian's account of how the fighting affected a small area on the Anglo-Welsh border; rather, they are a novelist's re-creation of the impact of the war on a community of ordinary men and women. Great historical events are not necessarily understood by the individual, but the suffering (or benefits) they may bring are certainly felt by him. The war, which occupies only a small part of this chronicle of more than eighty years, is seen from the viewpoint of the individual: ignorant, generally helpless, sometimes protesting.

'This Tribunal, having carefully considered your case . . .' The formula words are insultingly ironic. Only perfunctory consideration has been given to each man who has come before the committee.

the photo itself was unharmed The detail could be taken to symbolize the continuing strength, or at least survival, of Amos and Mary's marriage despite this latest crisis.

The World was Safe for Democracy As the capital letters suggest, this might have been a newspaper headline or an emphatic pronouncement made by some politician. In its context – we have just read details of Benjamin's maltreatment – the assertion looks ironic ('if this is how a democracy treats its citizens . . .').

Dardanelles In the eastern Mediterranean and site of one of the most famous campaigns of World War One.

Spanish influenza Many millions died in the outbreak which followed on the ending of the war.

Questions and assignments on Chapter XVIII-XXII

1 Why is Amos so hostile to the war? Explain how his attitude differs from that of the local clergyman.

2 Discuss the differences that emerge in these chapters between the twins' characters and interests, and show how the author demonstrates that there is still an indissoluble bond between them.

3 How are the English characters presented in this section of the novel?

Assignments

1 Write a dialogue between any of the members of the Military Tribunal, as described by Chatwin, discussing any of the 'cases' that come before it (in Chapter XXII).

Chapter XXIII

The war is over but it continues to leave its imprint on a number of the characters. There are the obvious victims, like the maimed veterans described in the next chapter; there are those like Benjamin or Jim the Rock who return physically and mentally scarred; and there are others whose lives are affected or distorted by what has happened. The next few chapters examine the aftermath of the war. Benjamin returns home, haunted by memories of the barracks; he 'seemed to have slipped back into childhood' and he fears all contact with a hostile adult world. Sexuality is a part of that adult world, and when Lewis strikes up a friendship with Rosie Fifield, his brother's jealousy is instantly aroused. Sullen, self-destructive behaviour is his means of protest. By contrast, Lewis's interest in Rosie appears as natural and inevitable as the return of spring; he is on the edge of adulthood at the turning-point of the seasons in 1919.

Spring came The season, obviously suggestive of growth and renewal in human as well as natural terms, has not been mentioned in the chapters devoted to the war.

'I'm coming,' said Benjamin An indication of his anxiety over his brother's friendship with Rosie; it is more powerful than his fear of leaving The Vision.

Chapter XXIV

This chapter describes the National Peace Celebrations, as they are mounted in Rhulen. Lewis's pursuit of Rosie Fifield is the reason for the twins' being there – it is no celebration for either. Chatwin uses the festivities as the occasion for comedy (of a fairly bitter variety) and implicit comment on the gap between the public rhetoric concerning the war and the reality as experienced by the private individual.

We are given a panoramic picture of the scene, as the victory procession moves from the town to Lurkenhope Park, where lunch and the Carnival Pageant are to be held. The picture is crowded, from the urchins 'blowing their pea-shooters' to the Brigadier at the other end of the social scale. But underneath the superficial high spirits and universal self-congratulation, there are less attractive features. Those who do most of the talking – Mr Arkwright and the Brigadier – are not those who have borne the weight of the fighting. The real wounded make a grotesque huddle in an open charabanc. The local Rhulen hero – the Bombardier 'who had rescued his commanding officer at Passchendaele' – is a pitiful figure, disabled and terror-stricken, imagining that the war is still on. In the face of this inarticulate suffering, the pomposity, complacency and patriotic generalities of the speeches are like salt rubbed into wounds.

Peace may have come but old animosities and differences still flourish. There is an early quarrel about the order of the various groups in the parade. The Bickertons' house party won't lower itself to lunch with the ordinary townspeople; evidently in the Brigadier's eyes the 'hoi polloi' (a phrase meaning 'common people', 'rabble', and suggesting his attitude towards them) are good enough to be sent out to fight and die, but not good enough to sit down to a meal with. Benjamin is spotted by one of his tormentors from the barracks, and he and Lewis are set on by a group of Army thugs. The warping effect of the cheap patriotism – or jingoism – of the occasion is shown by Rosie Fifield's handing Lewis a white feather. As a non-combatant, he is automatically considered to be a coward or shirker (although, ironically, Lewis had offered to take his brother's place in the call-up).

There is little real rejoicing in this 'celebratory' chapter. Rather there is vindictiveness, in the abuse directed at the supposed 'shirkers'; self-importance and ignorance on the part of the speech-makers; a painful frustration for Lewis when he discovers that Rosie now stays at the side of Reggie Bickerton. And the chapter closes on a note of acid irony with the disclosure of the death of the Bombardier: the local hero left out like a piece of garden furniture when the crowd ran for shelter from the rain.

flapper Term applied at the time to a girl dressed daringly and living frivolously.

urchins were blowing their pea-shooters at a Belgian refugee It was the German crossing of the borders of Belgium which caused Britain's entry into the war. The children's taunting of the refugee could be seen as a mildly ironic comment on the fact that, while nations make alliances between themselves, hostility or mockery between individuals of those nations may still thrive.

W.A.A.C. Women's Army Auxiliary Corps.

Rorke's Drift Site of famous battle (1879) in the Zulu War.

Land Girls Women doing agricultural work as part of the war effort.

Oddfellows Members of a secret charitable society.

Nurse Edith Cavell Famous martyr of World War One. Matron of a Red Cross hospital in Brussels, she was executed by German firing-squad (1915) for sheltering and helping in the escape of allied soldiers.

All the same, it was a right royal feed Perhaps the only note of unqualified approval in the whole chapter!

glissando A musical term, its meaning here is 'slide', a 'scale running from top to bottom'.

the Refugee, who stood and gaped blearily from under his beret The Belgian is either a little drunk or over-used to being pointed out as a representative of the 'weaker nations' on whose behalf the allies had been fighting.

the solicitor's black-market peccadillo Arkwright wasn't threatened by the starvation which menaced 'those whose lot it was to remain at home'. Like many others, he got round rationing restrictions by buying goods at higher prices on the black-market. The comment shows him to be a hypocrite.

Lewis began to tremble Because he sees Rosie with Reggie Bickerton.

Prince Ruprecht German Army commander.

a stuffed canary In place of the imperial eagle which is the proper topping for the Kaiser's (Emperor's) helmet.

sewiously, sewiously The author makes it impossible to take the Brigadier seriously from the beginning by giving him a comic lisp.

Vimmy . . . Wipers . . . Passiondale British version of French names; respectively, Vimy Ridge (1915), Ypres (site of several battles), Passchendaele (1917).

One went for days without a change of clothes In the context of the casualties, present and remembered, the Brigadier's 'suffering' seems insultingly frivolous.

'If I should die, think only this of me . . .' The lines are, in fact, from *The Soldier* by Rupert Brooke (1887–1915). The tone of the famous poem – one of gentle acquiescence in death and nostalgic patriotism – appeals to the Brigadier, even if he's ignorant of its real author.

'Poor Rupert' i.e. Rupert Brooke.

infewior animals . . . half-bweeds The Brigadier's speech degenerates into an absurd lecture on cattle-breeding, to the embarrassment of the other notables on the platform.

'The Battle of Om-dur-man' Anglo-Egyptian forces under the command of Lord Kitchener won a victory against the forces of the Mahdi at Omdurman in the Sudan (1898).

tableau-vivant Motionless scene presented by people in costume.

the Dove of Peace panicked and shredded its wings against the bars of the cage The detail indicates that the afternoon is not proceeding in the orderly way intended. By now there is something sour and ragged about the celebrations: it's one of the feathers of the 'Dove' (actually a pigeon) that Rosie presents to Lewis, a gesture not of peace but of jeering recrimination. Note that the chapter ends with a fight and a death.

the silver cigarette-case The dead man's grip on his 'trophy' provides a final, pitifully comic touch.

Questions and assignments on Chapters XXIII-XXIV

1 Describe Lewis's growing interest in Rosie Fifield, and the effect this has on Benjamin, as revealed in these chapters.

2 Show how the author illustrates the continued impact of the war even after it has finished.

3 What criticisms would you make of the speeches given by Mr Arkwright and the Brigadier in Chapter XXIV?

Assignments

1 Imagine that you are a reporter for a local newspaper attending the National Peace Celebrations in Rhulen. Write your account of the day.

2 As a researcher into the First World War, you interview two or three characters who appear in this section of *On the Black Hill* (for example, the Brigadier, a Conscientious Objector, one of the wounded veterans). Make a recording of the interviews, in a small group, or provide a written account of what is said.

Chapter XXV

The next two chapters deal with individual casualties of the war, Jim the Rock and Reggie Bickerton. This is not to say, however, that the focus is only on them or what they have suffered. The war was a catastrophe; the author stresses the misery it produced and does not search for any benefits in it. But most of the characters escape relatively unscathed. Life continues: families expand or contract; the Joneses begin to earn a modest financial security at the same time as their landlords, the Bickertons, start to run into money troubles; Jim the Rock recovers from his wounds and boasts that it was he 'who had won the war' (his suggestion that mules should wear gas-masks, prompted by his fondness for animals, is taken up by the High Command – the story has its humorous side); Watkins the Coffin demonstrates his vindictive nature once again; and so on. The narrative, tied to the advancing century, charts the growth (and decay) of individuals, families and groups. Inevitably, there are changes, movement and separations. In part these can be seen to have been produced by the war and the different sort of society which appeared after it – there is, for example, a stronger sense of family fragmentation (Jones, Watkins, Bickertons) than before – but the changes are in larger measure independent of outside events. As the novel progresses we see that they are indicative of a rhythm in human affairs, success following on failure, or a period of misfortune overtaking one of happiness.

moil Spoil (dialect word).
they turned away from the modern age The twins' – Benjamin's, especially – retreat into the world they know becomes more marked as a result of the war and its aftermath.
francophilia Love of France (Britain's war-time ally).
an Irish navvy, a Catholic The nationality, religious denomination, even the status (a 'navvy' is a labourer) of the father of Rebecca's child make her 'offence' even harder for Amos to accept.
Russian bonds Financial investments made in Russia, not recoverable after the 1917 Revolution.

Chapter XXVI

The chapter might be titled 'Rosie Fifield's story'. It explains how she comes to be living with her child in self-sufficient seclusion on a smallholding near The Vision. The account of her entanglement with Reggie Bickerton – crippled, deserted by his fiancée and his friends – evokes some sympathy for the man who had gone out in 1914 'with a head full of chivalric notions of duty to caste and country'. It indicates that all classes were affected in some degree by the war. Reggie's treatment of Rosie, however, shows him in a bad light. Although his need for her is understandable – she is the only eligible woman within reach and is not only vulnerable to his charm but also attracted by the gilded future he seems to offer her – he nonetheless uses his advantages (status, wealth) to manoeuvre her into his bed and, after she reveals her pregnancy, uses those same advantages to escape the consequences of his actions. Rosie's poor opinion of men is confirmed by his cowardly flight. There is a parallel between her retreat from the world and the twins' withdrawal into a narrower circle. Friends of a sort in childhood, they have suffered bruising contact with a hostile adult world and retired to lick their wounds.

Castor and Pollux Twin brothers in classical mythology – 'Heavenly Twins' because they were made into the constellation of Gemini. An echo of the flesh-and-blood twins in the novel is apparent here.
In her imagination, she saw the butler bringing in her breakfast-tray Rosie is attracted by Reggie's proposal. Marriage would mean a life of luxurious security. It's a mark of his desperation (and

unscrupulousness) that he 'proposes' to a woman so far 'below' his own class.

Lewis watched them for ten minutes Lewis sees that there is no place for him in Rosie's self-contained existence. Their tentative relationship was broken off by her affair with Reggie, and Lewis is too shy (and respectful) to attempt to resume it.

Chapter XXVII

The account of the auction, at which the farms belonging to the Lurkenhope Estate are sold off, is one of the most dramatic episodes in *On the Black Hill.* The chapter provides a good example of Chatwin's sheer narrative skill. Some suspense is introduced when it is revealed that the properties are to be sold on the open market, and that there is no guarantee that the Welsh families who have occupied them, perhaps over several generations, will be able to buy the places that they rightfully regard as their homes. When this question has been settled to the farmers' satisfaction – their ringleader, Haines of Red Daren, threatens to boot out of the room anybody who dares to bid against a tenant – and the sale appears to be going the way of the tenants, a new danger is introduced in the person of Watkins the Coffin. He has returned to pursue his vendetta against the Joneses and forces up the bidding on The Vision to a level far above that which Amos can afford. This exciting spiral of bid and counter-bid makes the climax of the chapter. The ending leaves us uncertain as to how Amos will be able to find the very considerable sum (£5,500) which pride and rage at his rival's intervention have forced him to offer.

Another element in this chapter is the resurgence of hostility and suspicion between the Welsh and English characters. There is comedy in the way the auction degenerates into a nationalist rally – but there is also real and justified anger at the high-handed behaviour of the English landlords and their representatives. The Estate's Trustees act with an obvious insensitivity – even with moral irresponsibility – towards those who have lived on and farmed their land for so long.

death-duties Tax levied on a dead person's estate; a proportion of its total value is paid to the government.

the bank-manager . . . foresaw no difficulty in securing a loan A clear indication of the new prosperity which has arrived at The Vision.

the twins both blushed They are embarrassed to be reminded by their father that he expects them to marry and produce sons, to whom the farm can be passed on. The Biblical terminology – 'Hand of God', 'seed' – suggests that Amos regards farming as a divinely appointed activity.

the hat she wore for funerals A mark of the sombre importance of the occasion.

He had recently lost his wife The detail, contributing towards a 'sketch' of Haines of Red Daren, is easily overlooked, but it is relevant to later events. Chatwin is meticulous in laying down small facts which are pursued at later points in the novel.

Amos broke from the circle to greet his former enemy Amos's wish to conciliate is shown, but on Watkins' side there is only hostility.

reserves If the bidding at an auction fails to reach the reserve price the item is withdrawn from the sale.

troubles enough in Ireland The Dublin uprising (1916) and subsequent agitation against the British presence in Ireland, a stimulus to Welsh resentment of English control of their affairs.

Chapter XXVIII

Once again it is Mary Jones who proves herself the stronger, more practical partner. While Amos retreats to his bed, shocked at the price he has been driven to offer in the auction, Mary goes to see Mr Arkwright to obtain a reduction in the price and then, when she fails in that attempt exploits her old connection with Mrs Bickerton to make a direct appeal for The Vision. She goes through the same process as she does in Chapter V, a futile approach to an agent followed by an appeal, woman to woman, that achieves her objective. Mary stands as the saviour of her family, or at least the family home. She saves The Vision by drawing on the well of class-solidarity and sympathy that exists in Mrs Bickerton who replies to Mary in terms that suggest that she is addressing a near-equal: 'Poor you! What an ordeal!' for example. But security is purchased at a price. Mary has to withstand an outburst of ingratitude from Amos: she is responsible for everything – good and bad – that has happened to them. He is furious that it was '*her* connections', 'her clever clever letter' that saved the farm – her influence makes him appear insignificant. The one thing he wants, which she can't obtain for him, is his daughter's return. He is reduced to the status of a 'frightened child'; Mary becomes a 'mother' to him as well as to the twins. She also has to deal with her own ambiguous response to Mrs Bickerton's letter. It offers salvation to her family, but it condemns her to spend the rest of her life 'in this gloomy house below the hill'. The Vision is home but it is also a kind of prison. Restless thoughts of travel, a new life, are prompted by the sprig of mimosa enclosed in the letter from the South of France. The bloom releases a scent but it also unlocks in Mary some long-repressed desire for 'warmth and ease', a return to the travelling existence that she had experienced with her father.

she had – had she not? – betrayed her class Arkwright's snobbery outdoes anything displayed by the Bickertons. Ironically, his employers have no respect for him (in the letter Mrs Bickerton refers to 'that awful Arkwright').

them two halfwits! The twins are abused, along with Mary. Amos fantasizes that he can bring Rebecca and her husband back, to take over the farm. He feels that his daughter is 'his' in a way that Lewis and Benjamin never have been.

Questions and assignments on Chapters XXV-XXVIII

1 Describe the partial break-up of the family groupings that occurs in these chapters. What conclusions do you draw from this?

2 How does the author balance sympathy and disapproval in his characterization of Reggie Bickerton (Chapter XXVI)?

3 What makes the auction of the farms a dramatic occasion?

Assignments

1 We are told that Mary Jones wrote 'letter after letter' to Mrs Bickerton. What sort of things would you have included in the final version?

Chapter XXIX

Amos's illness and his death in an accident are handled in the understated, matter-of-fact manner that is characteristic of the novel. At the start of the chapter he is laid out with a stroke; at the end he dies as a result of being kicked by one of the mares on the farm. Interwoven with this account of Amos's decline are two small stories: we learn that Arkwright the solicitor, one of the few genuinely unpleasant figures in the narrative, has been convicted and hanged for the murder of his wife; we also read of Merlin Evans, who makes a living by touring the hill-farms and hiring out his stallion to service the mares and who has some success in offering a parallel service to the local wives (sometimes with the connivance of their husbands who have 'an eye to fresh blood in the family'). It is a measure of the abundance of incident and character in *On the Black Hill* that these two figures, who might be thought interesting enough to occupy several chapters, are relegated to the background. The author juggles with contrasted elements: old characters are disposed of, new ones introduced. Through everything runs the thread of the Joneses' family history, but their history is never seen in isolation from the community which surrounds them.

it was she who ruled The Vision Mary takes over all aspects of the farm. In a sense, Amos's illness merely confirms her in the central position which she has long held in the hosuehold.

and the sparrows went on chattering Like other deaths in the novel, Amos's is described in a context which underlines the continuity of life and activity, whether on the human or the animal level.

Chapter XXX

Preparations for Amos's funeral interrupt but do not put an end to work on the farm. The twins recede into the background – we are not told directly of their response to their father's death – and it is Mary's reaction to the death of the demanding, moody man she lived with for twenty-seven years that concerns us. Mary's grief is repressed until after the funeral and then shows itself in ways that are both poignant and ironic. Her dedication to his memory ('She patched his jacket . . . laid a fourth place for supper') is touching in the elaborate forms that it takes. It is ironic that she should, after his death, copy those traits of his character which had 'once annoyed her most'. The bond between them is at its strongest when they are first married – and, perhaps, after his death. It is only then that the real extent of Mary's devotion to her husband is uncovered. We understand, looking back, how the marriage survived strain and crisis.

like crows at the lambing season The comparison is between the women in black clustered round the white corpse in its coffin and the swoop of crows on weak or still-born lambs. The simile is obviously suggested by the black/white contrast but there is a predatory, oddly unfeeling quality to it too – as if the mourning women were somehow 'feeding off' what they were gazing at.

This, she recalled, was custom in the valleys We remember that Mary is still a 'foreigner' in the valleys; its customs don't come instinctively to her.

table-turning or the techniques of spiritism Mary does not 'talk' to her dead husband through a medium or at seances, where bits of furniture might be moved around (table-turning) supposedly by the agency of spirits. Rather, her behaviour shows how she refuses to acknowledge that Amos is gone. She continues to repair his clothes, prepare his meals, and talk as though he were still with her (as, in a sense, he is).

the house began to look like a museum Mary's desire to keep everything as it was when Amos was alive is reinforced by the twins' natural conservatism.

Chapter XXXI

The chapter enlarges on the 'very disagreeable incident' in which Benjamin found himself temporarily suspected of the murder of Alfie, a simpleton who is the child of Ethel, 'sister' to Jim the Rock. This episode doesn't advance the narrative much, leading only to one of the periodic bouts of hostility between the two farms and perhaps confirming Benjamin in his suspicion of the outside world (the presence of the policemen who have come to inquire into what turns out to be an accidental death is a painful reminder of his arrest in 1918). The chapter, like many others in the novel, is complete in itself as a blending of character-sketch and miniature story. The short life-history of Alfie and his agony when Jim sells a clock – his 'one true friend' because its ticking makes him think that it is alive – combines comedy and pathos, without sentimentality. In addition, there is an implicit contrast drawn between the household of the Rock and the occupants of The Vision, both in this chapter and others. Where the Joneses are orderly and industrious in their lives, the Watkins exist in a (sometimes) cheerful disorder. Jim sells the clock for drink money, while Ethel makes 'no special effort' to find Alfie after his disappearance. Though fond of each other, the members of the Watkins clan are not bound by the same ties of love and need as are the Joneses. Despite the feuding between the two families – less marked now that Amos is dead and Watkins gone – they remain neighbours: their farms share a common boundary. However variable their relations they must continue to live side by side – like the twins, like the English and the Welsh.

it was Mary who saved the day Mary has the presence of mind and the tone of authority which convince the policemen that they have made a mistake.

Chapter XXXII

There is conflict in Mary's desires for the future of Benjamin and Lewis. One part, the maternal side, wants to keep them to herself, preserved from marriage. Just as nothing has been permitted to change in the house, so nothing must change the status of the twins – they should remain her sons, not turn into other women's husbands. Another side of her, however, acknowledges the need for continuity after she has gone: at least one of them must marry to provide the grandchildren who will take over the farm. This was Amos's preoccupation in his last years. She senses that Benjamin will never need a wife. He is, in effect, asexual, finding fulfilment in his closeness to Lewis. The latter, on the other hand, 'wanted a woman badly'.

An undercurrent of sexuality runs through this chapter. After Mary has sent her boys off to Rhulen Fair, with the instruction to 'pick the pretty ones', she falls into a day-dream 'of certain nights and mornings – in the bedroom with Amos'. We are reminded of the early strength of their physical passion for each other. At the Fair Lewis is split between his own needs and fear of his brother's disapproval. The desires and responses of the two young men are opposed here. Where Lewis is tempted by a performance of the 'Dance of the Seven Veils', Benjamin is repelled by the flesh on display, quantities of legs which remind him – significantly – of a visit to a slaughterhouse. Sexuality is for him something frighteningly repellent and dehumanized. When Lewis eventually meets up with a couple of girls, Benjamin joins the group only when he perceives that they pose no threat to his intimacy with his brother. Benjamin's watchfulness gives to their relationship at this point a stifling quality. Once again he is revealed as the more powerful of the two, and in the dominance of the 'weaker' partner there is an echo of the supremacy achieved by Mary in her marriage.

a momentous decision The reclusive nature of all their lives is indicated by the fact that an outing to a fair becomes an event of major importance. Mary sends them off like children, preparing a picnic lunch and waving goodbye.

Thomas Hardy Major English novelist (1840–1928). Hardy's works appeal to Mary because they have rural settings and because they describe a nineteenth-century world (in many respects The Vision has turned its back on the twentieth century). The novel referred to in this paragraph is *Tess of the D'Urbervilles* (1891), a tragic story of a beautiful country girl. Mary identifies with Tess, or at least with the jobs she does on the land.

Wessex Name given by Hardy to the area of England (South and South-West) in which his novels were largely set. The name was originally that of one of the Saxon kingdoms.

Hardy's 'coincidences' Hardy has sometimes been criticized for the crude nature of some of his plotting, dependent as it is on 'coincidences' which usually plunge his characters further into misfortune. Mary finds this feature irritating in *The Mayor of Casterbridge* (1886), a novel where the author's manipulation of events is particularly obtrusive. The other book mentioned is *The Woodlanders* (1887).

a little Tower of Babel In the Old Testament story (Genesis xi) God frustrated plans to build a tower as high as heaven by 'confounding' the language of the builders and making them unable to understand one another. A rather weighty comparison for an innocent helter-skelter, perhaps suggesting Benjamin's puritanical attitude towards the fair.

Mary . . . thanked him for bringing his brother home The gesture and the words hint that there is an unspoken understanding between mother and son. Lewis has been 'allowed out' to get a taste of the wide world, to have a mild sexual adventure, but every move on his part towards independence has been frustrated by Benjamin's presence. Benjamin returns him untouched, and Mary is grateful for it.

Questions and assignments on Chapters XXIX-XXXII

1 How does the author handle the death of Amos? What impact does it have on his family?

2 What do the characters, Mr Arkwright, Merlin Evans and Alfie add to this section of the novel?

3 Explain the contradiction in Mary's hopes for her sons' future.

4 How understandable do you find the Joneses' desire to preserve things as they always have been? Give reasons for your answer.

Assignments

1 It is obvious that the twins are as dependent on each other as ever. Can you think of other examples of such mutually dependent relationships from your reading (*Of Mice and Men* by John Steinbeck is a good example of a link between different kinds of strength and weakness)?

Chapter XXXIII

The chapter marks time. There are no overtly dramatic events here. Lewis and Benjamin expand their interests to include archaeology and treasure-hunting. They cast themselves in the roles of Christian martyrs or hermits, a romanticized version of the seclusion from the world which they already enjoy. Lewis's obsession with flight is now channelled into a preoccupation with the famous lady aviators of the late 1920s. These exotic women and their aircraft are equally out of his reach: perhaps that is why he idolizes them.

the Fair Rosamond Mistress to Henry II.
Froissart, Giraldus Cambrensis and Adam of Usk Medieval chroniclers, whose work was to produce a mixture of history and story-telling.
Crécy Site of battle (1346) in which English and Welsh forces under Edward III defeated a far stronger French army, partly through the use of the longbow.
Tomb of Tutankhamun Excavations at this famous Egyptian tomb continued for several years after its discovery in 1922. The public imagination was caught by the splendour of the tomb furnishings and by the 'curse' supposed to cling to anyone who entered it.
St David Patron saint of Wales.
St Dubricius Supposed founder of one of the Welsh bishoprics; according to one chronicler he crowned Arthur king of Britain.
anchorites Holy men who live in extreme simplicity, secluded from the world. We can see why this would appeal to Benjamin.
the Slump The crash of share prices on the Wall Street stock market in October, 1929, was the event that ushered in the Great Depression.
R 101 British passenger-carrying Zeppelin which crashed in France, while attempting a flight to India in 1930. Like the detail referring to the Slump, above, this reference marks the passage of the years.
Amelia Earhart The first woman to fly the Atlantic, in 1928.

Chapter XXXIV

The next few chapters cover the twins' entry into middle age. Lewis again experiences conflict between his desire for love (and sex), which would free him from the confines of his family, and the commitment to Benjamin and his mother, a commitment in which there is certainly love but also resentment and frustration. He falls for the widowed owner of a neighbouring farmhouse, Mrs Musker, 'an uncomplicated soul, who enjoyed having a man about the place'. Lewis, however, is restrained by his innate timidity from responding to her hints and when he eventually nerves himself to claim her he discovers that Haines of Red Daren has usurped his place. The violent story of the illegitimate baby, murder and suicide bursts through the narrative. After Mrs Musker's death, Lewis tends her grave – for which he has bought a simple memorial cross – and holds himself in some way responsible for what has happened to her. Threatened by Haines, he turned away from her door and did not call in the police.

Chatwin treats the episode without sensationalism. The two killings are described in a matter-of-fact fashion and, as with other (non-violent) deaths in the novel, we are not allowed to forget that such events, however shocking, take place within the context of a community that has the capacity to absorb and endure (look, for example, at the exchange between the Coroner and Mrs Yapp in which the difference in styles of speech works to comic effect). There is contrast here, too, between the aggressive passions of Haines and the wistful devotion of Lewis, as he chooses an inscription for Mrs Musker's cross or clears her grave of weeds. His ineffectual chivalry and decency are at least as important as the dramas of birth and death.

Benjamin shot an anxious glance at his mother Benjamin is so alertly jealous that any compliment Lewis pays to a woman is noticed and treated as a threat.

He had a terrible temper This has already been suggested in the auction scene (Chapter XXVII).

a 'touch of the tarbrush' The phrase suggests that there has been some racial mixing somewhere in Haines's family history – a prejudiced way of accounting for his temper.

Bethel Hebrew word meaning 'house of God'.

Chapter XXXV

The contrasting households of The Rock and The Vision are set before us. The habits and eccentricities of earlier days become more marked with the passing years. The squalor and inertia of life at The Rock come in part from the ruling impulse in Jim's gentle nature: 'his reverence for animal life'. Not merely is he unwilling to slaughter any of his stock but he adds to it by buying the broken-down and unwanted animals left over at auctions. Similarly he adds to the farm equipment by a process of haphazard accumulation – rather as the children rejected by others have found their home with the Watkins. The farm implements are rusted and unused, the animals are diseased, the children are sick. The crisis comes when 'Little Meg', Mrs Musker's child (by Jim, as it transpires), falls dangerously ill, and Mary Jones is summoned to give assistance. Once again, the lives of the occupants of the two farms are shown to be intertwined.

At The Vision, Mary's thoughts turn towards her own death. The patchwork quilt (first mentioned in Chapter I) that she works on, so that the twins will have something to remember her by, has a symbolic value: its materials (black velvet, 'gaily-coloured calico') evoking different stages of her life. To mingle the materials so that they form a ptachwork, to 'marry' one to another, suggests the attempt to make something whole out of diverse elements. It could be interpreted as a metaphor for Mary's need, now that her life is nearly over, to find unity and completeness in that life. Mary is not morbid in envisaging her death, for she also looks to the future of her farm – unlike the inhabitants of The Rock. With Benjamin, she shows a provident concern to extend the boundaries of their territory, to find security in owning more and more land, an understandable preoccupation when we remember how close the family came to losing the farm. Lewis, however, grows more aggrieved: he considers that his interests are being ignored.

'We shall do nothing about it.' The long and bitter feud between the Joneses and Watkins began with thefts from The Vision. Mary prefers to let the pilfering go unreported rather than provoke fresh trouble.

'I shall only go to one funeral now' Mary is being realistic (compare with the morbid relish of Hannah Jones knitting her last pair of socks).

Questions and assignments on Chapters XXXIII-XXV

1 What interests do Benjamin and Lewis pursue (Chapter XXXIII) and what do these tell us about their characters?

2 What contrasts are there between The Rock and The Vision?

3 There is tension between Lewis and Benjamin in these chapters. Which character do you feel more sympathy for? Give your reasons.

Assignments

1 Write an account of the murder and/or inquest (Chapter XXXIV) as it might have appeared in the local newspaper.

2 Make some diary entries, as they might have been written by Benjamin, covering some of the events of this period.

Chapter XXXVI

The two new characters who appear in this chapter are intruders: English, 'artistic', sophisticated, and dangerous. Although credible – they are sketched with Chatwin's customary eye for the telling detail – they justify almost too well the rural prejudice against the 'outsider'. The Lamberts are pretentious and frivolous. Their lives are seen as aimless and fundamentally false. The affected extravagance of their speech is contrasted with the earnest sincerity or incomprehension of the Jones twins. Husband and wife (we are told that they 'shared a conspiracy of gin, but not a bed') exploit Benjamin and Lewis. Nigel wants to use Benjamin as the 'model' for a series of sketches; Joy sets out to seduce Lewis because he represents a challenge. Neither has any genuine respect for those on whose lives they intrude. Both take from the community, Joy in particular seizing whatever takes her fancy: furniture, ornaments, and in the end Lewis's virginity. She pursues her chosen twin and, although Lewis is naturally not unwilling, the impression remains that he has fallen victim to a calculating woman who has taken him in with a persistent and methodical campaign. Her reward is the bottle of gin, a private bet made with her husband ('You had him?' he queries when she returns); for Lewis, the experience is disorienting. Benjamin's uncontrollable jealousy and his brother's panic-stricken response lead to the temporary break-up of The Vision.

the Spanish Civil War Lasted from 1936 to 1939. The Republican (government) forces were opposed by the rebels led by General Franco. The Fascist dictatorships in Germany and Italy gave assistance to Franco. The Republicans had support from, among others, an International Brigade made up of left-wing opponents of Fascism drawn to Spain by the ideological nature of the conflict. Writers such as George Orwell took part in the fighting. Nigel Lambert is obviously capitalizing on his hearers' ignorance in order to boast about his role.
a Picasso etching The world-famous Spanish artist (1881–1973). Possession of one of his works, in the 1930's, signifies the 'modernity' of Joy Lambert's state.
She despised Nigel for lacing his plummy voice with working-class slang Mary is instinctively hostile to the strangers who pose a threat to her sons. Nigel's use of slang suggests the essentially patronizing nature of his approach to the 'peasants' – or 'Earlies' as the couple condescendingly refer to them.
Berlioz French composer (1803–1869).
'Him was none too keen on it' Predictably, Benjamin is unwilling that Lewis should go on the riding expedition.
'Very romantic! Rather damp!' Contrast the jaunty dismissiveness of her tone with the effect of the experience on Lewis.

Chapter XXXVII

For the second time in his life Lewis leaves The Vision and finds a job elsewhere. He is drawn back towards his home but Mary tells him he cannot yet return because of the strength of Benjamin's jealous rage. It takes the death of their mother to unite the twins – for good. Only an event so absolute can bring them together. It says much for the restrained power of Chatwin's narrative that Mary's death, although foreshadowed for several chapters, is dealt with in a few lines but is nevertheless perceived as the climactic event in the twins' lives. In Chapter I we are told that 'they lived for the memory of their mother'. A fine example of the effects that can be achieved by understatement – by what is not said rather than what is overtly stated – can be seen in the final section of this chapter. Almost wordlessly, Lewis and Benjamin make up their parents' bed after Mary's funeral and climb into it together. They have literally taken the places once occupied by Mary and Amos. The image of union which is an aspect of marriage is now theirs (look again at the opening paragraph of the novel), although there is of course no sexual undertone here. From the moment of Mary's death the twins are all in all to each other: brothers and 'husband and wife'. This happens in September, 1939 – the outbreak of the Second World War. But the twins are so engrossed in the memory of their mother that history passes them by.

'If thy right hand offend thee . . .' The quotation (from Matthew 5:30) concludes, '. . . cut it off, and cast it from thee'. It was with his right fist that Lewis struck his brother (end of previous chapter). He has evidently attempted to mutilate himself – there is 'a vicious purple scar' around his wrist – because of his extreme sense of guilt at having hit out at Benjamin. This self-inflicted punishment indicates how seriously Lewis regards his offence and how literally he interprets Biblical teaching.

'Thank heaven for that!' Mary is shocked at what Lewis has done to himself, but she is also relieved because it is a sign of guilt at his behaviour towards Benjamin. She herself is profoundly disturbed by the rift between her sons.

Mary wore herself out with housework Aware of her impending death Mary works to get everything 'in order'.

Images of India A return to childhood memories. The 'cloth-bound bundle' is a body borne to cremation (see note on Burning Ghats in Chapter VI).

the latest news from Poland Hitler's advance into Poland, which provoked Britain's declaration of war on Germany.

'He's come,' she repeated Mary refuses to die until both her sons are by her bedside. The picture is as she envisaged it (Chapter XXXII).

Chapter XXXVIII

This chapter covers the period (nearly six years) of the Second World War. Its impact on life at The Vision is much less severe than that of the Great War, as the opening sentence indicates. Indeed, in some ways, the ripples of the conflict as they reach Lewis and Benjamin are exciting, even beneficial. The arrival of troops from the United States or the Dominions (Australia, India) is an exotic intrusion. Benjamin adds more land to their possessions and the twins acquire a German prisoner-of-war to help them farm it. He joins their household, is given a place at their table, is unofficially 'adopted' by them and, in his turn, adopts their country as his new home. The only overtly dramatic event of the war is the crash of a plane near The Vision, a small disaster that Lewis is unhappy to have missed.

Other narrative threads are taken up during this time. A friendly but tentative relationship is re-established between Lewis and Rosie Fifield, and the Bickertons' history is brought up to date. New figures are brought into the community, some (like Manfred Kluge) welcome, others (the Lamberts) not, but the reintroduction of characters from the past provides that impression of continuity which is such an important aspect of *On the Black Hill.*

the Coventry Raid The German air-raid (in November, 1940) devastated the city.
Home Guard Volunteer force, made up of those beyond the age of or exempt from military service.
her clock of the Heavenly Twins The gift from Reggie Bickerton – a reminder of the past for Rosie (and also for the reader).
She unpacked the basket Lewis's gift of food, rationed during the war, is a way for him to re-establish the connection with Rosie, a justification for his visit. It also underlines his good nature.
'It's no good' Rosie is tempted by the protection and care that Lewis offers, but mistrust of men rules out any closer relationship.
D.T.s Delirium tremens, condition (affecting the brain) caused by alcoholism.
her mother who was interned in the South of France As an enemy alien, Mrs Bickerton would have spent the war years confined in the place that she had made her home.
with the indulgence of doting parents The twins, without other outlets for their affection, treat Manfred as a 'son'. He has been badly treated by his father and his mother is dead; he is, in effect, an 'orphan', out of love with his fatherland. As a prisoner-of-war in Wales he has landed on his feet.
a bold headline The headline refers, not to the ending of the war in Europe (that is relegated to a smaller item on the same page), but to the conclusion of another sort of conflict: the landing of a salmon after a 'three-hour struggle'. The choice of news – a parochial item being given precedence over something of major historic significance – is a humorous reflection of local priorities. World War II does not appear to have been a catastrophic experience for the neighbourhood.
the mushroom cloud above Nagasaki An atom bomb was dropped on the Japanese city on 9 August, 1945, three days after the first had been dropped on Hiroshima. They brought about the unconditional surrender of the Japanese. The twins' response to this event, the beginning of the nuclear age, is their 'identical nightmare'.

Questions and assignments on Chapters XXXVI-XXXVIII

1 What criticism of the Lamberts is there in the description of their characters and activities (Chapter XXXVI)?

2 How effective do you find the author's treatment of the death of Mary Jones?

3 Compare the impact of the Second World War with that of the First on the community presented in the novel.

Assignments

1 Imagine that you are one of the 'outsiders' presented in these chapters. Write an account – as one of the Lamberts, as one of the foreign troops stationed in the area (even as Manfred, the German P.O.W.!) – of what you see and hear.

Chapter XXXIX

Lotte Zons, like other fresh characters introduced in this section, comes to The Vision as a result of the upheaval in Europe. She is a Jewish refugee from Vienna, who escaped shortly before the outbreak of war and endured a lonely exile's life in London. Her friendship with Lewis and Benjamin springs from two sources, her own isolation and a professional interest in the subject of 'twins who had never separated', something that she had made a study of in pre-war Vienna. Her academic jargon baffles the two but, since all the questions are posed in terms of friendly enquiry (compare her approach with the condescending exploitation of the Lamberts), she eventually wins them over. Her appearance allows the author to look at the phenomenon of twinship in a detached manner. More important, her curiosity enables Lewis and Benjamin who are not naturally articulate, to express and explore aspects of themselves and their relationship with each other that would otherwise have gone unspoken. Lotte's assertion, for example, that 'many identical twins were inseparable – even in death' pleases Benjamin because it conforms so exactly to his own feelings. Lewis's responses are more complex and ambiguous. To Lotte he can say what he would never say to his brother: that he resents the fact that Benjamin was his mother's favourite; that he cannot help speculating on the life he might have had – might still have – if Benjamin were no longer there. When he says this he is 'close to tears', and the tears are perhaps of frustration as much as of potential grief at Benjamin's death.

Apart from being a listening ear for the twins, Lotte Zons exists in her own right. She has her own history, with its sufferings and compensations. Her love of England, growing from her reading of literature, is cruelly disappointed during the wartime years in London. It is only when she reaches Rhulen, and travels along 'leafy lanes unchanged since the time of Queen Elizabeth', that her search for this imagined Eden is satisfied. We may remember that Benjamin found a kind of paradise in his surroundings. In addition, there is an affinity between the Jewish refugee and Lewis, delicately suggested in closing paragraphs of the chapter. An inscription on a memorial, commemorating a 'maede', 'no man's wyffe', touches her and her plight touches Lewis, the twin who has never found the completeness and fulfilment in the closed family circle that have come to Benjamin. His tentative approach to her is characteristically chivalrous and gentle.

Jane Austen The famous novelist (1775–1817) who represents, for Lotte, something quintessentially English.
the age before Sarajevo i.e before the First World War.
Belsen Film of the concentration camps first revealed to the public the full horror of the Nazi treatment of the Jews and other groups.
something in her manner had reminded him of Mary This explains the twins' receptiveness towards their visitor.
Holy Thorn Type of hawthorn, with religious-mystical associations.
Offa's Dike A great earthwork, probably defensive in purpose, running from north to south Wales, named after the Anglo-Saxon king in whose reign it was built.
Owen Glendower Welsh leader who fought against forces of Henry IV.
'monozygotic' Coming from one egg.
'Something like London, I expect' Benjamin's answer to Lotte's question as to how he imagines 'Hell-fire' is, in part, a joke but it reflects his profound distrust and fear of city life and its supposed values – or lack of them.
pectoral cross Cross worn on the chest.
the fiasco of the third Lewis's relationship with Joy Lambert.

Chapter XL

This chapter provides an account of the immediate post-war years at The Rock. In its squalor the household has appeared to be in a perpetual decline; now it is on the edge of collapse. There are two deaths, and 'Little Meg' is taken into hospital. The one 'responsible' member of the unofficial family is Sarah (daughter of the miller's wife – see Chapter XXV), who has always 'kept her eye on The Rock and made it her business to see they never starved' even after going off to live with a haulage contractor. In a sense, life at The Rock is a disordered and exaggerated version of the twins' existence at The Vision. They preserve the past and are deeply conservative or traditional in outlook (the one exception being Lewis's hankering after new farm machinery); the Watkins live in a kind of fossilized chaos, in which nothing is ever cleaned or discarded. Animals – and people – remain untreated in illness, because the Watkins lack the resources or, in their deep hostility to the world, are unwilling to seek help from outside. Meg refuses to be taken into hospital until the situation becomes so serious that there is no alternative. All this Chatwin recounts without condemnation. A few characters apart, mostly the English ones, he does not judge. The shape, a sometimes distorted one, of the hill-farmers' lives is conditioned by landscape and their often harsh conditions and upbringing. He gives credit to the good, decent impulses of these people, even if the results are occasionally ruinous, as with Jim's determination never to slaughter any of his animals. Similarly, the wariness shown towards strangers and the outside world is respected; it is frequently shown to be justified. There is, too, admiration for the stoical endurance of suffering, self-inflicted as some of it may be.

Knowing her to be light-fingered Like Mary Jones, the grocer allows some petty theft, not merely to avoid trouble, but out of kindness.

Chapter XLI

As the story approaches the present its tempo increases. Over a decade is covered here, and for Lewis and Benjamin it is a period of both advance and consolidation. Prosperity comes to The Vision, allowing Lewis to buy two tractors. The twins, however, have never learned to live in anything but a simple, unextravagant fashion. Their accountant is amazed to discover that £20 is their estimate for 'pocket money' for a *year*! Although respectful – even reverential – in their attitude towards the furniture of their past, they are in no way materialistic. Nor, in a sense, do they work for themselves. The brothers' early lives were dedicated to their mother; they worked for their father, then lived for her. The painful anxiety of their late middle-age is that all of this may go for nothing: what is the point of ownership 'if the one thing you lacked was an heir?' The deaths of many of their older neighbours bring them closer to awareness of their own deaths. The Vision is theirs in trust, but there is nobody to whom their lives' work may be safely and naturally entrusted.

Lewis loved his tractor The way in which Lewis's tending of the tractors is described suggests a diversion of his sexual instincts – when he gets another one he considers it too splendid to use but gazes at it like 'a little boy peeping into a brothel'.

Mr Nasser An indirect reference to the Suez Crisis (1956). Nasser, then President of Egypt, nationalized the Suez Canal, an action that provoked an abortive military intervention by Britain and other nations. The episode was widely seen as a final fling by Britain as a colonial power, and split opinion in the country – hence the accountant's comments.

the place went up in flames The destruction of the Castle perhaps signifies the withering-away of the old Establishment, as represented by the Bickertons.

'more English than the English' The phrase suggests that the German has adopted English habits and pursuits more wholeheartedly than the English themselves.

his establishment Manfred's factory-farming methods are not to the twins' taste.

Questions and assignments on Chapters XXXIX-XLI

1 What purposes are served by the introduction of Lotte Zons?

2 What impression do you receive of life at The Rock during this period?

3 What consolations and worries do the twins face as they begin to grow old?

Assignments

1 We are told that Lewis and Benjamin's sixtieth birthday 'was almost a day of mourning'. Write a dialogue between the two which indicates some reasons for this.

Chapter XLII

The appearance of Mrs Redpath and her young son Kevin is a godsend to the twins, for she is their niece and the boy their great-nephew. Their anxieties as to who will inherit The Vision are resolved within a few years when the farm is willed to the boy. This doesn't come as a surprise; we already know from Chapter I that this is the course of events. By opening the novel (in 1981) with the twins, in their eighty-first year, confident that The Vision will be passed on within the family, Chatwin perhaps reduces the element of uncertainty or suspense in this part of the narrative but he gives an air of inevitability, almost of fatalism, to what occurs. This must happen – the arrival of an 'heir', his growing up to receive the farm – because it is laid down in the beginning (of the novel). There is some doubt at first, however. Benjamin, more watchful than his brother, thinks that Mrs Redpath is 'bent on their money', a suspicion that is partly justified. In later chapters Kevin develops in such a way as to cast a shadow over his suitability as the successor to the Jones twins. Their first introduction to Kevin is to see him perform in a nativity play. The setting is the occasion for some gentle humour as the children blunder through the drama. For Lewis, and for Benjamin who is initially sceptical, the play is a moment of magical revelation. Just as the Three Wise Men (with their chocolates, bottle of shampoo, etc. substituting for the gifts of the Magi) arrive to catch a glimpse of the promised child, so too do the twins see their 'promised child' in the boy with 'an oval face with grave eyes'. Chatwin keeps the chapter earth-bound – the infant Christ is a plastic doll, Kevin gets threatened by his mother – and avoids the scene's latent sentimentality. That Lewis and Benjamin are moved to tears by the sight of their great-nephew tells us how powerful is their need for an heir, how gratefully they welcome the possibility of a future.

Chapter XLIII

Kevin rapidly becomes the twins' favourite. They treat him 'like a little prince' and, through him, they relive the pleasures of their own childhood. Introduced to Meg the Rock, he is at first entranced by the strange vision of her feeding the birds, then – realistically – horrified by the dirt and oddity of The Rock. What stands out in this chapter is not so much Kevin's smooth progress through boyhood and the twins' love for him, as the image of Meg, scraping together fragments of courtesy to welcome her visitors, so unused to kind treatment that Kevin's present of a cake prompts her to ask how much she owes for it, and so frightened of Jim that she asks them to take the remains: 'I wouldn't want Jim to catch me with a cake.'

He saw lambs being born . . . The twins introduce the boy to all sides of farm life.

Croziers of young bracken A crozier is a bishop's crook; the curling shape of the bracken suggests the image.

The stump moved Meg is at first indistinguishable from the landscape. To Kevin she is 'lovely', the 'Bird Lady'; she is closer to animals than to humans.

Chapter XLIV

Kevin's entry into the twins' lives had earlier been seen as 'a gift from Providence'. But after they have made out their will in his favour, they begin to grow disappointed in him, his laziness, his impatience with their old-fashioned farming methods. If the novel has been successful in convincing us of the value of the Jones twins' lives, their integrity, their passionate commitment to their home, land and past, then we should begin to share something of their unease. At one point it seems as though the narrative is going to conform to what is something of a clichéd situation: the irresponsible 'heir' who wastes an inheritance that has been laboriously built up by others. But this doesn't happen in *On the Black Hill.* Kevin turns out, in the end, to be an affectionate, dutiful nephew. Lewis and Benjamin cannot foresee this; we can, because Chatwin has already told us (in Chapter I) of the twins' sense that time has run in a 'healing circle' at the the end of their lives, something they would not feel if they did not have confidence in the future. At the moment (the early 1970s)

Kevin appears as a threat; that he ultimately redeems himself points not only to the optimism that underlines much of the novel but also to the unpredictability of human nature.

Stamp Duty Tax payable on legal transactions.
Moved to silence The twins are taken back to the childhood shared with Rebecca. Mrs Redpath's greed and insensitivity are shown by the manner in which she bundles up these 'sad, crumpled relics', taking them as her entitlement.
the Hippies An incongruous presence in the valleys, they're a source of scandal or amazement.

Chapter XLV

The tone of the opening half of this chapter is one of gentle reminiscence. The friendship between Nancy, who is now the sole bearer of the Bickerton name, and the Jones twins (no one will inherit their name either) is something that would not have been possible earlier in their lives. Now they are all survivors, and barriers of class disappear. They have a fund of shared memories to draw on; there is an echo in their meetings of the friendship between their mothers. Memories and pictures of India, symbol of exotic distance, link the two families in an oblique fashion. Like the twins, Nancy hoards material from the past; unlike them, she has to make do with living in circumstances which don't match the grandeur of her youth (a handful of rooms must now hold 'the relics from fifty-two rooms of a castle'), whereas Lewis and Benjamin have reached a degree of financial security unattainable in their younger days. Their territory has grown, as the Bickertons' fortunes have waned. It is one of the many incidental subtleties of *On the Black Hill* that the social changes of this century which have led to the gradual displacement of the 'older' families by representatives of a different class are hinted at in this way.

Age and innocence make the twins vulnerable. An unscrupulous antique-dealer – another 'outsider' – in effect robs them of 'a relic of Mary's', a writing cabinet. This explains why they 'were terrified of . . . antique dealers' (Chapter I). It is not of course the loss of the valuable object as such that distresses them enough to make them ill; rather the fact that it is one of the many strands that link them to their late mother. They feel agitated too by the antique-dealer's cynical manipulation.

'China or Indian?' The question asked by Mrs Bickerton three quarters of a century before. A humorous touch: the twins are bewildered by the query, as their mother was.

'And it was all my fault, you know?' Nancy had lectured her brother Reggie on the 'scandal' of his involvement with the village girl Rosie. She blames herself for the fact that they never married.

'Antiques' and 'Antiquarian' An antiquarian is someone who studies relics from the past. Lewis, always the less sharp of the twins, assumes that the stranger has a benevolent interest in their possessions.

out of politeness The antique-dealer's sharp practice looks the more heartless when set against the hospitality he receives.

Nostradamus Sixteenth-century French astrologer, whose books of rhymed prophecies gained him a wide audience. His obscure predictions are still credited. The shifty Mr Cole mentions Nostradamus' forecasts in order to unsettle the twins; he then takes the cabinet away for 'repair'.

'And Jim's gone!' The unself-conscious monologue which takes up the rest of the chapter is a tribute of sorts. The dying man's final rambling words – on the care of the animals, and on plums – achieve a bizarre, near-poetic quality, as they are faithfully reported by Meg. It never seems to occur to her to feel sorry for herself.

Chapter XLVI

Meg the Rock proves her entitlement to the name by which her farm is known. The other 'children' of the household have dispersed but, after the death of Jim, she hangs on, much to the fury of Sarah and Lizzie. Her eccentricity and detachment from reality – Sarah claims she's 'losing her marbles' – are, in part, comically rendered (see her account of 'being attacked by strange men.'). But Meg's affinity is to the natural world; for the human one she feels only fear or hostility. Her imaginative identification with animals is so complete and intense that she can believe herself to be at one with badger cubs, with hawks; she curls up to sleep with a black cat; food is left for her, by arrangement, and when it is stolen Meg has no recourse but to starve (like an unfed animal). Characteristically, the author treats this strange figure with some warmth; her peculiar life – not so much sub-human, as passed beyond human reach – is endowed with a value, with a magical, near-religious significance (she believed a woodpecker to be 'a messenger from God and sang His Praises'). There is a contrast in this chapter between the wrangling of the adults over possession of The Rock and the childish simplicity of Meg – although she is sufficiently shrewd to realize when her 'sisters' are trying to curry favour with her.

'Space Invaders' The reference 'places' the episode in the present – such references are a means by which the author can avoid too much explicit dating in the novel.
Official Receiver Person appointed by a court to look after a property, the ownership of which is disputed.
with a black cat for company Meg is a latter-day witch.

Questions and assignments on Chapters XLII-XLVI

1 Explain the difference between the twins' first impressions of Mrs Redpath and Kevin, and how both are eventually won over.

2 What is your impression of Meg the Rock? Use quotation and reference in your answer.

3 In what ways do Lewis and Benjamin find themselves rediscovering aspects of their past, in their seventies?

4 Through use of revealing detail Chatwin suggests the changes – social, cultural – that have overtaken the community depicted in the novel. Discover, in these chapters, some of that detail and discuss it.

Assignments

1 As part of a project at your school, you have gone to interview one (or both) of the twins at The Vision. You can ask them about any aspect of their lives (although they may choose not to answer!). With others, produce a recording of such an interview; alternatively, write an account of it.

Chapter XLVII

The introduction of Theo the Tent into the novel, and into the twins' lives, brings forward a figure who is simultaneously old and new. Theo is that recognizable type from the late 1960s and 70s, the drop-out. He had originally joined a Buddhist group, which, it is hinted, exploited him for his money and his strength. Now he 'drops out' from that inauthentic organization, too, and lives alone and in extreme simplicity. In Buddhist terms, Theo is searching for The Way, the path to enlightenment. He has come 'to believe that all men were meant to be wanderers'. The nomad as the archetypal human figure appears elsewhere in Chatwin's work. Here it is enough to note that Theo's beliefs stand in contrast to the practice of most of the other characters: Lewis and Benjamin, and many more, could be described almost as anti-nomads. They live their lives within a constricted circle. The notion of moving away from the landscape of their birth fills them with fear of the unknown (see the Introduction for further discussion of this topic). However marked the contrast between the rooted manner of their lives and the wandering existence enjoyed by Theo, there are also points of contact here. Theo's self-contained, self-sufficient way of life is not so different from the twins' attempt to preserve their independence, to keep the world at arms' length. Theo's love of nature and his rejection of materialism put him in tune with Meg the Rock; he is entranced by the 'music of her voice', he feels there is 'something sacred about her rags'. He becomes her 'fancy man'. In the neighbourhood of the Black Hill Theo finds remoteness and hospitality, a community which is fundamentally tolerant and welcoming, set apart from the 'destructive world beyond'.

Dharma The Law (Buddhist term).
mandalas In Buddhism objects symbolizing the universe. These, and other paraphernalia in the Monastery, seem to Theo flashy and worthless when set against the beauty of natural objects.
Tao Tê Ching Ancient book of philosophy and guidance.
haikus Three-line Japanese poems with pre-set number of syllables per line.
a ten-penny piece Neither Theo nor Meg have – or wish to have – any concept of the value of money. What she gives him for helping to set her house in order is a token of appreciation; he accepts it as if she were offering him 'a fortune'.
Benjamin [was] **far from happy to think she was one of the Watkineses** The two households have frequently been at odds, yet their fortunes have also been intertwined. The marriage between the 'heir' to the Jones twins and one of the The Rock's 'children' underlines this link.
Theo and the twins were devoted to one another Lewis and Benjamin's capacity for friendship with those very different from themselves (Miss Bickerton, Theo) is one of the most notable and attractive features of their old age.
bodhisattva Buddhist term, meaning one who delays fulfilment in order to assist others.
Who doth ambition shun The lines are from Shakespeare's *As You Like It*. They have an obvious relevance to Theo's situation. Much of the play takes place in a rural setting which is part paradise, part a testing ground for the characters – an echo of the landscape in *On the Black Hill*.

Chapter XLVIII

This chapter, describing the twins' birthday flight, is one of the climaxes of the novel, just as it is a climax in the long lives of Benjamin and Lewis. Notice how Chatwin keeps the reader in the dark in the same way that the brothers are kept guessing as to what Kevin's treat is. There are the fussy preliminaries to the flight, signing insurance forms, Benjamin's understandable panic. Kevin's affection for his uncles is clearly revealed. Then the plane lifts off the ground, and the twins' spirits soar with it. For Lewis, at the controls at last, it is a moment of delight, of fulfilled aspiration: 'all the frustrations of his cramped and frugal life counted for nothing'. His life-long obsession with aeroplanes is satisfied in 'ten magnificent minutes'. The twins come down to earth at the end of the chapter with a tangible memento of the great experience, an aerial photograph of the house where they have passed their lives. That they quarrel about where the photograph should be placed on the wall shows how the experience has earned its position in their family history.

To look down on a landscape from the air is to see it whole, in a way that it can never be glimpsed at ground-level. The twins see The Rock and The Vision side by side, they see their land, as they have never seen it before. There is a symbolic value which is implicit in the flight. Much of the novel is given over to the struggle between disparate halves in a relationship of inter-dependence (husband and wife, brother and brother, Wales and England); the two sides can grow together, they can fall apart. From the air the twins catch sight of an image of wholeness – for Lewis it is an experience which somehow justifies what he has endured throughout life, and even Benjamin conquers his fear in enjoyment. And this 'vision' of their 'Vision' and its surroundings is granted to them through one of the technological developments of the twentieth century, a century which, as Chatwin shows, has both blessed and cursed those who have lived through it.

Mr Lindbergh One of the most famous of the early aviators, Charles Lindbergh made the first non-stop flight between New York and Paris (1927).

Chapter XLIX

It is 1980. The twins are now in their eighty-first year. There are ominous signs of a hard winter. Benjamin and Lewis are encouraged to go to the Chapel for the Harvest Festival. Like the Festival, the chapter itself is a kind of gathering-in. There is a sense of completion and reconciliation, as various figures are drawn towards the Chapel. The two Lessons that are read in the course of this rich service are full of significance, the verses from Ecclesiastes testifying to the dominance of the seasons in all natural life, the sense that there is an appropriate time for all human activity, whether happy or mournful; the passage from the Book of Revelation, read by Theo, points towards a mystical concern with a spiritual world beyond human reach, the Holy City. The minister's eloquence touches poetically on the impermanence of life.

Lewis's death – not witnessed by Benjamin, but nevertheless sensed by him in his intuitive identification with his brother – is described indirectly, with flat, matter-of-fact detail. The accident, neither shocking nor really unexpected (Lewis is accident-prone), is to be seen in the context of the rest of the chapter which succeeds in imparting an impression of things – season, year, individual lives – drawing to a close. This is an occasion for sadness but, like the Festival celebrated in the Chapel, also a time for gladness at what has been achieved or endured. Chatwin does not allow this crucial chapter to dissolve into religious sentimentality. Lewis's death is not turned into a dramatic centre-piece; its effectiveness is gained through understatement. And the autumnal season begins in the most mundane way, with the arrival of the new minister to get a donation from the Jones twins for the renovation of his dilapidated Chapel.

the needle's eye The reference is to the famous verse (Matthew xix:19), 'It is easier for a camel to go through the eye of a needle, than for a rich man to enter into the kingdom of God.' Benjamin is thinking of his own exit from life to rejoin his beloved mother; when the farm has been safely entrusted to Kevin, death becomes an easier prospect.

a rainbow arched over the valley The significance of the rainbow – God's promise to Noah in the Old Testament, and sometimes symbolizing union – scarcely needs to be pointed out. The 'flock of black rooks beneath it' are in sinister contrast.

Chapter L

As in many novels, this final chapter provides a kind of 'catalogue' of the fortunes or whereabouts of some of the principal characters. Benjamin, Kevin and his wife, Theo, Meg, Rosie Fifield – the book leaves them at this point. This bald statement, however, does not indicate anything of the emotional force achieved at the end of the novel. We see that Benjamin has been broken by his twin's death; in a sense, he has died too. He spends his only happy time in the graveyard staring at 'his reflection' in the shiny tombstone; the image he sees is at once himself and Lewis. There is no difference between them. The account of his dazed grief is short – and pitiful. The other older characters continue to live, unmoved (and, in Rosie's case, unmovable). Elsewhere there is change, as Theo resumes his nomadic existence and Eileen (the new mistress of The Vision) begins, with an unfeeling lack of tact, to sweep away the relics of the Joneses' lives. Furniture and pictures, lovingly amassed over a century or more, are sold or swept away. The ending is ambiguous. The changes are regrettable but it may be that they are also inevitable. Throughout the novel we have understood that what gave the objects (so meticulously traced through the years by the author) their value was not so much an intrinsic worth as the significance attached to them by earlier generations. Now those generations have gone, and a new family wants new things. The final sentence is similarly ambiguous. The 'fatal accident' witnessed by Rosie Fifield is the death of a hang-glider – the kind of incident that might have been included in Lewis's scrapbook of aerial disaster. We are reminded of the twin who always wanted to fly and who, just before his death, succeeded.

Questions and assignments on Chapters XLVII-L

1 What is the role of Theo the Tent in the closing stages of the novel?

2 Why is the flying episode (Chapter XLVIII) important?

3 How does Chatwin prepare us for the death of Lewis in the penultimate chapter?

4 How effective do you find the final chapter? Give reasons for your answer.

Assignments

1 *On the Black Hill* contains many references to famous events. Make a list of some of them, with dates if possible, and indicate the stages reached by Benjamin and Lewis beside each item (i.e. the twins' ages, what they were doing, etc.).

Bruce Chatwin's art in *On the Black Hill*

Introduction

A complex novel has several aspects and can be approached by different routes. At the most basic level, you might examine it as a story and see how the narrative is organized. The author's use of characterization, his style, the themes dealt with in the book – all of these will be components of the work. But we should remind ourselves at the beginning that a novel, if it has any claim to complexity or profundity, works as a *whole*, that the parts it is made up of cannot be studied entirely in isolation from each other. An obvious parallel is with an engine, each component of which has to function properly for the machine to operate as it should. Engines, however, are constructed to a predetermined pattern, and if they are doing the same job will differ little from one another; a novel – or any work of art – on the other hand will always bear an individual stamp and the things that make it different from other novels are likely to be more marked than the similarities.

Plot

The story of *On the Black Hill* is the history of its principal characters and their families, the Joneses, Watkins, Bickertons, as they move through almost a hundred years. The plot is provided by these and other figures and the developments and changes in their lives. The narrative therefore does not seem to be imposed on the characters from outside but to spring largely from their own strengths and weaknesses, their individuality. When Mary Jones reads Thomas Hardy (Chapter XXXII), a novelist she likes for his rural settings, she finds that 'Hardy's "coincidences" had begun to grate on her nerves'; Hardy often seems to manipulate his characters and situations too obtrusively so as to make some (usually ironic) point. It is a danger that Chatwin avoids, and we don't have the sense of an overbearing authorial presence in *On the Black Hill* manipulating events so as to produce an ironic or tragic intensity. Instead, the narrative appears to take a natural, plausible course. The characters seem to develop 'by themselves'.

Characters and history

This impression of the characters' autonomy, the impression that they have lives of their own which the author is 'merely' chronicling, is a result of Chatwin's approach to his subject-matter. The first question we must ask, therefore, concerns the way in which his figures are developed. As already noted in the Introduction, one of the shaping forces is the course of history itself: the effects of two wars and the slower and less dramatic pressure of social and cultural change. An example of the latter is the way in which the Welsh hill-farmers gain gradual independence from English domination. They buy themselves free of their landlords (Chapter XXVII) and some of them grow relatively prosperous. The poverty and insecurity that are such evidence features in the early life of Amos Jones and his parents have given way, by the end, to a fair degree of material comfort for his descendants, although it must be said that this is not something to which Lewis and Benjamin attach much importance. Conversely, the ascendancy enjoyed by the English is a thing of the past: the Lurkenhope Estate is broken up, the Bickerton family dead or dispersed (only Nancy survives, to renew friendship with the twins). The power of the old landlords is diminished, as that of the farmers is increased. The development of the novel reflects the way in which, in the later twentieth century, the rigid system of class and authority – based on birth, education and ownership – has been modified by historical progress.

History or culture, however, leave their marks. We can see this in the way a number of people cling to their land: Meg, the last of the Watkins clan to live at The Rock; Rosie Fifield, who refuses to be moved into an almshouse in her eighties – 'You'll have to drag me by the feet' is what she tells the District Health Officer (Chapter L); the Jones twins themselves, especially Benjamin who is always anxious to extend the boundaries of their land. This limpet-like loyalty to territory has its roots, no doubt, in the historical/cultural worries of a people who could at any time be turned out of their houses at the whim of their landlords. Historical circumstances, in other words, have produced traits of character, such as stubbornness or defensiveness. Similarly, the arrogance of some of the English is in part a product of the situation that history has placed them in, and their exploitation of that situation. Reggie Bickerton's high-handed treatment of Rosie, Arkwright the solicitor's malevolent snobbery, these would not flourish as they do were it not that social or cultural factors have encouraged their growth.

History, of course, doesn't altogether explain character, even if it helps to illuminate some aspects of it. In a chronicle like *On the Black Hill* which covers several generations, we see how families make their own moulds into which succeeding generations are expected to fit. Parents shape and influence their children, both consciously and unconsciously. Amos, for instance, deliberately sets out to turn his boys into farmers from their earliest years and is determined they will not be 'mollycoddled'. Mary, by contrast, has aspirations for the twins (expecting a single boy, she thinks, 'He'd grow up to be a statesman or a lawyer or a surgeon who would save people's lives') and does her best to provide the formal education which Amos considers to be a waste of time, even a threat. Each is trying, as parents often do, to make the children in his/her own image. Neither succeeds outright. The twins do take over and extend The Vision, as their father desired, but they frustrate Amos in his dearest wish of providing grandchildren to carry on the good work, and by the end of his life he can think only of his absent daughter as a potential heir. Mary is disappointed in her ambitions, particularly as regards Benjamin, but finds great consolation in her old age from the presence and love of her sons in her household. All this could be interpreted as ironic comment on the way in which the attempts of one generation to shape the next, misfire. Plans and expectations are not fulfilled, but there are sometimes blessings which have never been looked for.

A more important 'shaping' of their lives, however, occurs at a deeper level. It is apparent early on that each son takes after one parent, and after Mary's death this is underlined by the fashion in which Benjamin assumes the 'feminine' role (doing the cooking, mending, taking care of the money) while Lewis continues the more 'masculine' part. These roles are adopted in a sketchy form when both are boys (see especially Chapter XIII) and are implicit in their youngest days (we are told that Lewis was the 'stronger one' even at birth). Their individual characteristics are as much an inheritance from their parents as the pieces of furniture which they treasure so carefully throughout their lives. This is not to suggest that Chatwin has created his princiapl figures by the crude expedient of transferring character traits from parent to child, but the partial 'modelling' of a child on a parent demonstrates that the notion of 'inheritance' goes beyond the straightforward passing-on of land or possessions, or physical features. It is one of the means by which the novel gains in density and continuity.

No other family is described in such detail as the Jones family, but the history of the inhabitants of The Rock also shows how a family-style group creates its own pattern to which succeeding generations will correspond or against which they will react. The poverty, sometimes cheerful but squalid as well, the resolute isolation from the world, the hostility towards outsiders, and the occasional moment of relief when a kindness from outside breaks down the barriers, the haphazard rescuing of children or animals – these features of the Watkins's lives recur throughout the book. Even if the 'children' escape from their environment, as Sarah does from The Rock (like Rebecca from The Vision), their behaviour can be interpreted as a reaction against the attempt to impose a pattern on them. This 'pattern' is a complex framework of habit and expectation, class and situation.

Pattern and rhythm

We might note at this point that pattern and rhythm are significant aspects of *On the Black Hill.* Both words suggest recurrence. At the simplest level, the very work on the land in which many of the characters are engaged, is dependent on the predictable cycle of the seasons, and the tasks appropriate to a particular time of year. What Lewis and Benjamin have to do on the farm towards the end of their lives is essentially the same as they did at the beginning. On a more complicated level, patterns emerge within families and between generations as different members echo or contradict one another. Mary and Benjamin share an obsession with purchasing land; Jim and Meg are alike in their distrust of humanity, and helpless love for animals; Lewis and Benjamin reflect each other in looks, although they are at odds in many other ways, and each is identified with (as well as standing opposed to) a different parent. In a related way, we can discern a pattern in the fact that an affectionate closeness will, like electricity, leap a gap between generations: old Sam the Waggon's befriending of the twins, and their own attachment to their great-nephew, suggest a re-establishment of links, a continuation of the pattern which can be both threatened and also confirmed by time. Time changes and destroys, but it renews too. Sixty years separate Lewis and Benjamin from Kevin, but across the gap of years they see in him a physical resemblance to their beloved mother and his very existence offers them the assurance that their lives' work hasn't been wasted, because there is someone to inherit the farm. Much space in the novel is given to description of the seasons, in all their distinctness and variety but also in their predictable return; such a cycle in the physical world provides a parallel with the history of the families. They change, the individuals within them grow and die, but certain shapes and patterns remain fairly constant.

We can see, then, that Chatwin shows his characters to be formed by various pressures: history, family, the environment, conscious attempts to pull them in one direction, and instincts of which they may scarcely be aware that push them in another. This may seem to give to *On the Black Hill* a rather deterministic view of human development. In other words, the manner in which people come to be what they are is shown to be something largely outside their own control, the result of a combination of environment, heredity, historical circumstance, social or cultural factors. In a sense, this is true. The story is shaped by the birth and death of the Jones twins (even though Benjamin survives, it is sadly obvious that he has nothing to live for and has, in a way, 'died' with his brother). The novel begins at the end, as it were, with the brothers in their eighties, jumps back in time to describe the events preceding their births and then works steadily and chronologically through the years until it reaches the present. The shape of the book is the shape of individual lives, two in particular, and the course of the individual life is enevitably laid down in its large dimensions. Everybody is subject to time. The stress on the passing of the years in the novel adds to the impression that a lot of what we think of as composing 'character' is not so much a matter of choice as of necessity.

This fairly deterministic view of human nature is often identified with a pessimistic or tragic outlook, yet although there are pessimistic and tragic elements in Chatwin's novel they do not give the book its dominating tone. The reason for this is that the characters are shown to be embedded in time, but not submerged by it; they are not helpless or insignificant victims of the unrolling years. They have some freedom of choice, and they are accorded dignity and weight by the author. Lewis's attempts to break away from his home can be seen as an example of this. On two occasions (during the First World War and after his seduction by Joy Lambert) he actually leaves The Vision; at other times, a potential marriage or romantic attachment that would take him from mother and brother is hinted at. We know that such an 'escape' is doomed before it begins – he is anyway half-hearted in his efforts to break away – but Chatwin invests these moments with an intensity and immediacy that underlines the acute division of loyalties that Lewis experiences. His struggles are not futile or without value, rather they demonstrate his strength and sensitivity. The novelist doesn't condemn him as a 'failure', any more than Benjamin is acclaimed a 'winner' for keeping his brother by his side. As for the other figures, there are gains and losses in the way of life that choice –and inevitability – have created for them. The fact that *On the Black Hill* ends on a note of decay and death (and inescapable change as new occupants move into The Vision) doesn't undermine or diminish the worth of the lives that have been chronicled in its pages. In a sense, the novel could be seen as an assertion of the value of the ordinary, the historically 'insignificant'. It is the narrative of people whose lives are spent on the margin (or border) of history, where the things that matter are not the events that get recorded in newspapers and history books. Nevertheless, what does happen – birth, death, marriage, family crises and reconciliations – has a universality that rises above a particular place or period.

Completeness

At the start of this section I said that we should be careful to see the book as a whole, not as an assembly which can be simply dismantled into its component parts of character, theme, style, etc. This consideration, which should be borne in mind when studying any complex novel, has special relevance to *On the Black Hill* because the book seems to work towards images of wholeness, completion or union. The opening words of Chapter I are,

'For forty-two years, Lewis and Benjamin Jones slept side by side, in their parents' bed . . .'. The final chapter describes Benjamin's melancholy vigil over his brother's grave, one half of the 'block of shiny black granite' being left blank to take the final inscription when the surviving twin joins Lewis in a last sleep 'side by side'. This phrase well describes the theme of doubleness, or duality, which is one of the principal aspects of the novel. Benjamin and Lewis live, day and night, 'side by side', as their parents did.

Further examples of living 'side by side' are easy to see. The Vision and The Rock share a common boundary and, however bitter the feud grows between the occupants of the two farms, they must continue to live next to each other. Church and chapel co-exist. They worship the same God, but membership of one or the other carries with it a train of associated loyalties (to class, nationality, upbringing) that have little to do with pure religion. At best, the adherents of one form of worship regard their opposites with tolerance, at worst with hostility (ironically the outbreak of World War I is the occasion for a truce between church and chapel, when the two denominations unite in their enthusiasm for fighting). When Amos switches from chapel to church (Chapter III) or Mary goes in the reverse direction (Chapter XVII), each crosses a significant border from one piece of spiritual territory to another. The religious landscape may be continuous – the one God, the same sacraments, a common language of worship – but there are profound local differences between the two sides.

This observation could also be applied to the real, tangible landscape of England and Wales. The countryside, obviously, stretches unbroken from one nation to another and the exact location of the border is not important (although it is 'said' to run through the staircase at The Vision). But Chapter X clearly shows the topographical features of the 'Welsh' walk to be quite distinct from the 'English' one. The more important differences are not geographical, but are those connected with power: economic dominance, together with a kind of cultural confidence, are the property of the English in the early twentieth century. Although, by the close of the novel, the Welsh have much more control over their own lives, there is still the need for them to assert their distinctness and nationality (we are told that the minister of the local chapel was, in the 1980s, 'a Welsh nationalist of extreme views'). Yet the two nations share a border, they speak the same language, are subject to the same laws; their histories are inextricably interwined. Neither nation can escape the other. They are, helplessly, neighbours, forced to live 'side by side'.

Duality

We can see from the above, various types of duality or doubleness – in religion, in landscape, history, culture and experience. A more refined definition of this theme of duality might be found in the phrase 'difference in sameness'; two religions in one, two histories in one, etc. On the individual level, and more profoundly, this term applies to Benjamin and Lewis, even to the married couple Amos and Mary, who are both 'at one' yet (sometimes) at odds. They are distinct individuals, linked by a marriage which, despite the strains imposed on it, survives their lifetimes. One of the unifying ideas in the book is therefore the concept of union itself, the bringing-together (by history, circumstance, choice, or birth) of disparate elements and people.

This theme is most extensively explored in the figures of the twins. By their very existence, they go towards making actual the paradox of being simultaneously two people and one person. Like the 'Greek pair, Castor and Pollux ... (they) had both popped out of the same egg,' as Lotte Zons tells them (Chapter XXXIX). Benjamin, in particular, is always threatened by the potential loss of his other 'half'. Without Lewis he is himself 'lost' – literally so, when he disappears in a snow-storm (Chapter XXI), almost, it would appear, as a way of summoning Lewis home. At the same time, Lewis, the stronger of the brothers is constantly sensitive – to the point of rawness – to Benjamin's reactions. This goes deeper than emotional attachment. In Lewis's absence, Benjamin 'suspected him of stealing his soul'; or again, 'How could you believe in an immortal soul, when your own soul, if you had one, was the image of your brother across the breakfast table?' (page 193). Terms such as 'closeness', 'mutual dependence', do not adequately summarize such a relationship. Sometimes it seems as though Lewis and Benjamin are one person sundered in two, each half always aware of the split. In the person(s) of the twins Chatwin can develop the theme of unity in doubleness to its limit.

It should be noted, however, that union isn't won without effort, that indeed it is not always wished for by either side. Church and chapel, England and Wales, The Vision and The Rock, all exist in a state of enforced proximity, but the links between the 'halves' are frequently under stress. In each 'match' there is material for conflict, sometimes for outright hostility. We see in almost every chapter how religious denominations, two kinds of nationalism, neighbours, married couples, brothers, all can fall out, the tension in the relationship between the 'halves' being increased by their very closeness. Such relationships, too, are rarely between equals: the balance of power is constantly shifting, as one side prospers or achieves a kind of ascendancy at the expense of the other. Examples multiply throughout the novel. Amos and Mary are for much of the time engaged in quiet struggle, over the way the children should be brought up or the household should be run (in the early days of the marriage Amos is made very uncomfortable by his wife's attempts to introduce middle-class habits in the domestic routine. Later Mary takes control of the finances, and uses those middle-class connections to save The Vision). Even between Lewis and Benjamin easy co-existence is not always possible. Lewis is resentful of the manner in which his brother, and mother, restrict his life; they hamper his 'escape', they prevent his getting new farm machinery; and such resentment is natural and understandable.

Despite the often overt hostility between the various 'halves', there is a balancing impression that both sides have a need for or something to offer one another. The Joneses do what they can for the feckless inhabitants of The Rock; except at the height of the feud, they are good neighbours. A web of obligation and kindness is spun ('She [Aggie Watkins] never forgot an insult and she never forgot a kindness'). Practical charity weathers the years. Lewis, always the more neighbourly and sociable of the twins, still looks after his old friends at the end – 'old Miss Fifield the Tump had only to send a message with the postman, and Lewis would drive the tractor over with a load of bales' (Chapter I). The outbreak of the First World War demonstrates the automatic assumption by the English that they have a right to call upon the Welsh, even if such a call is represented in the novel as exploitation of the vein of patriotism that still exists in the Welsh nation. That the twins, together with their mother and father, have an overriding attachment which is far more binding than any of the factors that divide them scarcely requires underlining.

Division can also be seen as a creative rather than a negative force. Each 'side' may bring to a relationship, a union, complementary qualities which, taken together, might point towards an ideal whole. Amos's masculinity finds its counterpart in Mary's femininity; Benjamin's household talents discover their complement in Lewis's more masculine concern for the outside world. One twin directs himself to a life of domesticity (and inertia), the other dreams of distance (and movement). On a larger stage, the warm eloquence of the 'chapel' is balanced by the scholarly aloofness of 'church'. Welsh culture, which can sometimes appear parochial, is set beside an English tradition which offers a wider scope for the individual. The English family most thoroughly characterized in *On the Black Hill*, the Bickertons, has the money and resources to travel, to enjoy a more leisured life than is available to their Welsh neighbours. Stillness is poised against movement (the figure of Theo the Tent most completely embodies the nomadic existence which stands at the opposite pole to the static lives of the Joneses or Watkins). Opposition, balance, even mutual need – all these hint at the image of completeness which is such an important element in the novel. It may not be possible to achieve wholeness; it may not be desirable, because in doing so individual identity (of religion, nationality, culture, character) would be diminished or lost; but it is the state or condition to which the novel as a whole seems to aspire. The drift of *On the Black Hill* is in the direction of harmony and reconciliation, although full weight is at the same time given to individuality and distinctness.

Style and structure

The style and structure of *On the Black Hill* are inseparable from its content. Because the book covers a large span of time – a century in less than 250 pages – and includes several major characters, as well as dozens of minor ones, Chatwin's method is necessarily impressionistic; that is, for any scene or event he provides sufficient touches of detail for us to imagine the whole. We are told only what is important, and the book does not have the leisurely or digressive quality of, say, a Victorian novel. The mention of historical or 'cultural' detail ('the flight of Monsieur Blériot', 'he kept foul-mouthing a Mr Nasser', 'A man and a girl were playing a computer game') sums up a period. A single chapter can contain anything from a few days to ten years. The method is that of a chronicle, highlighting the significant moments and passing rapidly over the intervening gaps. Chatwin does this with such assurance that, for the duration of the novel, he persuades us that he is describing real events, real people. And because the work is so firmly rooted in the history of this century, the author is able to rely on the reader's co-operation in the construction of his 'fiction'. At some stage in the story, the reader, whatever his or her age, will come to a bit that is recognizable; the background, whether it is to do with the wars, or the social developments afterwards, will grow familiar. If the course of the novel is likened to a train journey, travelling by a fixed route (from the late nineteenth century to the late twentieth), then at some moment we will look out of the window and recognize the scenery, since it is the same landscape that we ourselves have passed through. The universal factors – birth, death, family division and reconciliation – are played out against an unwinding panorama of years which has, by the end, more or less reached the point where we are now.

The impressionistic, darting style of the book is echoed in its structure. The short chapters and brief paragraphs give an air of intensity and concentration – each statement counts, has something to say with economy and precision. Take as an example this passage (from Chapter XXXIX) in which Lewis is looking at a memorial in a churchyard with Lotte:

> Lewis stooped to recover the pencil; and he too recalled the misery of his first loves, and the fiasco of the third. He squeezed her hand and pressed it to his lips.
>
> She withdrew it gently.
>
> 'No,' she said. 'It would not be correct.'
>
> After high-tea, she took Benjamin aside and told him, in no uncertain terms, that he was going to buy Lewis a tractor.

If we've followed the development of character with any attention we should be able to understand the wistful chivalry of Lewis's gesture here, its delicacy and melancholy. There is an unstated pressure behind the moment. Lotte's refusal of him is sad but inevitable (she cannot come between the twins or, perhaps, turn her back on a lifetime as a spinster) but she can at least urge Benjamin, who controls the household expenses, to buy Lewis a tractor as a touchingly incongruous gesture of compensation. As elsewhere in the novel, as much is left unsaid as is stated. Chatwin's art is of the kind that depicts character with swift but careful strokes of the brush, without a laborious accumulation of speculation and commentary, and this spare, undemonstrative method is appropriate to the lives of most of the figures in the book.

Nature

A similar delicacy and exactness typify the descriptions of the natural world. Almost every page offers evidence of the author's eye and ear for the landscape (shape, colour, sound) that encompasses the events he brings to life. Here are two short examples:

> At the end of April there were pink buds in the orchard, and a vizor of cloud above the mountain. (page 35)

> Below, the river splashed against the boulders in mid-stream, and big trout lazily flicked their fins in the deep green pools. Pigeons cooed, and he could hear the *toc-toc* of a woodpecker. (page 112)

The first example comes from the account of the first year of Mary's marriage, a year that is balanced uncomfortably between delight (physical passion, the expectation of a baby) and the difficulty she has in accommodating herself to the grimmer features of her new life (her husband's moodiness, the austerity and strangeness of farm life). Both of these contrasting aspects are suggested in the first sentence, the fragile strength of the 'pink buds', with their connotations of hope and growth, being opposed to the more sinister overtones of the phrase, 'a vizor of cloud'. The more relaxed quality of the second passage – 'splashed', 'lazily flicked', 'cooed' – fits the context, as Lewis is about to renew his friendship with Rosie Fifield and there is an atmosphere of temporary relief after the hardship of the First World War. Such passages reinforce mood or echo events taking place on the human stage.

As a final point, however, we should be aware that the landscape doesn't exist simply for human purposes, whether as farmland or as a device for the author to convey atmosphere and tone. Chatwin does not 'use' the natural world in this rather functional fashion. Again and again throughout *On the Black Hill* we see that nature is celebrated for its own sake, as part of a total environment which contains individuals, animals, crops, trees, and the earth that supports them all. It is a place, a specific location, that gives to the novel its title; and as it is the Black Hill which dominates the (Welsh) view from the windows of The Vision, so it is the landscape as a whole which is the source of life in the novel and the place to which all will return after death.

General questions

1 Explain and discuss the difference of 'church' and 'chapel', and the importance of both in the lives of the characters in *On the Black Hill.*

Outline specimen answer

One of the most important distinctions in the novel is that between the two religious denominations. Amos and Mary each belong to both, at different times. In early stages (beginning of the century) membership of one or other also carries implications of class or national loyalty ('Church-folk, same as Amos and Mary?' is the first question Aggie Watkins asks about the young twins); even towards end (1980s) local minister is identified with Welsh nationalism. 'Church', roughly speaking, is 'foreign' institution to Welsh; 'chapel' is 'home', Amos is suspicious of/overawed by clergymen – Mary's father, her friend Reverend Tuke ('Bloody heathen!' muttered Amos). These two clergymen presented as stern, distant, scholarly figures. For Mary, on the other hand, 'chapel' is unattractive at first – she finds one minister 'grotesque'; his 'views on the Bible were childlike' – she's perhaps a bit snobbish about the religious institution of her adopted country. Later, though, she discovers real consolation in 'chapel' life, a warmth and lack of pretence that 'gives me great comfort'. Importance of both shown by frequent references to clergymen and ministers in novel. Two significant events – Amos's first encounter with Mary (Chapter III), harvest thanksgiving (Chapter XLIX) which brings all surviving characters together – occur respectively in 'church' and 'chapel'. Chatwin suggests that religious dimension is necessary aspect of life, even if this doesn't manifest itself in formal westernized fashion (Theo the Tent is dedicated to mystical search for meaning in life). Religion, or rather its representatives, can be comic; they're not above criticism (e.g. their attitude towards war, towards Conscientious Objectors), but novel as a whole does endorse concept of a spiritual/mystical realm underpinning everyday life. (Note also the reclusive lives of twins, particularly

Benjamin, who 'vowed himself to chastity' – like a hermit, or medieval saint.)

2 How important is the natural world in *On the Black Hill*? Discuss, with examples.
3 'The English figures in *On the Black Hill* are presented in clichéd terms; they are either arrogant or hypocritical.' Do you agree?
4 Why does Chatwin make his central characters twins?
5 As a reporter for the local paper (*The Rhulen Gazette*?) you have the job of interviewing one of the older characters (in the 1980s) on the subject, 'Wales as I remember it'. Write your report, or, with others, record such an interview.
6 'The most important element in *On the Black Hill* is the landscape.' Comment.
7 Imagine yourself to be Sam the Waggon, returning to visit The Vision towards the end of Lewis and Benjamin's lives. Write, with stage directions, the conversation that might follow, with particular attention to the changes that have occurred.
8 'Chatwin's art relies on understatement.' Discuss.
9 Examine the themes of duality and unity in the novel.
10 What impact do historical events have on the figures in the novel?
11 If you had to adapt *On the Black Hill* for television, film or stage you would have to be selective in what you dramatized. Everything that happens in the book can't be contained within a couple of hours. Which incidents would you select, and why (remember that the most dramatic events are not necessarily the most revealing)?
12 We are told that the twins 'turned away from the modern world' (Chapter XXV). Why do they do this? What features of the 'modern world' might make you 'turn away' from it?
13 What aspects of Chatwin's style are especially striking? Illustrate with examples.
14 What do the minor figures contribute to the novel?
15 Take the part of Kevin, and write an account of your uncles as they appeared to you when growing-up. This could also be done as an oral exercise, one person taking the role of Kevin, another that of a questioner.
16 Do you feel that the Welsh characters are 'better off' by the end of the novel than their equivalents were at the beginning? Give reasons for your answer.

17 Do you feel that any aspects of the novel – for example, its discussion of family ties, difference between nations – apply to aspects of your own life?
18 Why is the book titled *On the Black Hill*?
19 Take an episode from the book (the twins' appearance before the Military Tribunal, the auction of the tenant-farms) which involves a number of people. Using the novel as a basis, produce stage directions and some dialogue and dramatize the epoisode in a group. Allow for some improvisation.
20 What have you gained from studying *On the Black Hill*?

Further reading

Other titles by Bruce Chatwin:

In Patagonia (Picador, 1980).

The Viceroy of Ouidah (Picador, 1985).

Songlines (Picador, 1988).

Pan study aids Titles published in the Brodie's Notes series

Edward Albee Who's Afraid of Virginia Woolf?

W. H. Auden Selected Poetry

Jane Austen Emma Mansfield Park Northanger Abbey Persuasion Pride and Prejudice

Anthologies of Poetry Ten Twentieth Century Poets The Poet's Tale The Metaphysical Poets

Samuel Beckett Waiting for Godot

Arnold Bennett The Old Wives' Tale

William Blake Songs of Innocence and Experience

Robert Bolt A Man for All Seasons

Harold Brighouse Hobson's Choice

Charlotte Brontë Jane Eyre Villette

Emily Brontë Wuthering Heights

Bruce Chatwin On the Black Hill

Geoffrey Chaucer (parallel texts editions) The Franklin's Tale The Knight's Tale The Miller's Tale The Nun's Priest's Tale The Pardoner's Tale Prologue to the Canterbury Tales The Wife of Bath's Tale

John Clare Selected Poetry and Prose

Gerald Cole Gregory's Girl

Wilkie Collins The Woman in White

Joseph Conrad Heart of Darkness The Nigger of the Narcissus Youth

Daniel Defoe Journal of a Plague Year

Shelagh Delaney A Taste of Honey

Charles Dickens David Copperfield Dombey and Son Great Expectations Hard Times Little Dorrit Oliver Twist Our Mutual Friend

Gerald Durrell My Family and Other Animals

George Eliot Middlemarch The Mill on the Floss Silas Marner

T. S. Eliot Murder in the Cathedral Selected Poems

J. G. Farrell The Siege of Krishnapur

W. Faulkner As I lay Dying

Henry Fielding Joseph Andrews Tom Jones

F. Scott Fitzgerald The Great Gatsby

E. M. Forster Howards End A Passage to India

E. Gaskell North and South

William Golding Lord of the Flies Rites of Passage The Spire

Oliver Goldsmith Two Plays of Goldsmith: She Stoops to Conquer; The Good Natured Man

Graham Greene Brighton Rock The Human Factor The Power and the Glory The Quiet American

Willis Hall The Long and the Short and the Tall

Thomas Hardy Chosen Poems of Thomas Hardy Far from the Madding Crowd The Mayor of Casterbridge Return of the Native Tess of the d'Urbervilles The Trumpet-Major The Woodlanders

L. P. Hartley The Go-Between The Shrimp and the Anemone

Joseph Heller Catch-22

Ernest Hemingway A Farewell to Arms

Susan Hill I'm the King of the Castle

Barry Hines Kes

Aldous Huxley Brave New World

Henry James Washington Square

Ben Jonson Volpone

James Joyce A Portrait of the Artist as a Young Man Dubliners

John Keats Selected Poems and Letters of John Keats

D. H. Lawrence The Rainbow Sons and Lovers

Harper Lee To Kill a Mockingbird

Laurie Lee Cider with Rosie

Thomas Mann Death in Venice & Tonio Kröger

Christopher Marlowe Doctor Faustus Edward the Second

W. Somerset Maugham Of Human Bondage

Gavin Maxwell Ring of Bright Water

Thomas Middleton The Changeling

Arthur Miller The Crucible Death of a Salesman

John Milton A Choice of Milton's Verse Comus and Samson Agonistes Paradise Lost I, II

Bill Naughton Spring and Port Wine

R. O'Brien Z for Zachariah

Sean O'Casey Juno and the Paycock
The Shadow of a Gunman and the Plough and the Stars

George Orwell Animal Farm 1984

John Osborne Luther

Alexander Pope Selected Poetry

J. B. Priestley An Inspector Calls

J. D. Salinger The Catcher in the Rye

Siegfried Sassoon Memoirs of a Fox-Hunting Man

Peter Shaffer The Royal Hunt of the Sun

William Shakespeare Antony and Cleopatra As You Like It Coriolanus Hamlet Henry IV (Part I) Henry IV (Part II) Henry V Julius Caesar King Lear Love's Labour's Lost Macbeth Measure for Measure The Merchant of Venice A Midsummer Night's Dream Much Ado about Nothing Othello Richard II Richard III Romeo and Juliet The Sonnets The Taming of the Shrew The Tempest Twelfth Night The Winter's Tale

G. B. Shaw Pygmalion Saint Joan

Richard Sheridan Plays of Sheridan: The Rivals; The Critic; The School for Scandal

John Steinbeck The Grapes of Wrath Of Mice and Men The Pearl

Tom Stoppard Rosencrantz and Guildenstern are Dead

J. M. Synge The Playboy of the Western World

Jonathan Swift Gulliver's Travels

Dylan Thomas Under Milk Wood

Flora Thompson Lark Rise to Candleford

Anthony Trollope Barchester Towers

Mark Twain Huckleberry Finn

Keith Waterhouse Billy Liar

John Webster The Duchess of Malfi The White Devil

H. G. Wells The History of Mr Polly The War of the Worlds

Oscar Wilde The Importance of Being Earnest

William Wordsworth The Prelude (Books 1, 2)

William Wycherley The Country Wife

W. B. Yeats Selected Poetry

GCSE English coursework: Prose G. Handley and P. Wilkins

GCSE English coursework: Drama and Poetry: K. Dowling

PAN STUDY AIDS

C. Beswick and P. J. Downes
French £2.95

The contents of this Study Aid include: revising grammar, revising vocabulary, exam preparation, translation from French, prose composition, comprehension, essay writing, oral tests, dictation, verb tables.

A complete guide to preparing for O level, School Certificate and equivalent examinations in French, written jointly by two teachers and examiners in French.

David Shotter
German £2.50

The contents of this Study Aid include: revising grammar, revising vocabulary, exam preparation, translation from German, prose composition, comprehension, essay writing, oral tests, dictation, verb tables.

A complete guide to preparing for O level, School Certificate and equivalent examinations in German, written by the principal author of *Deutscher Sprachkurs*.

Derek Utley
Spanish £1.95

The contents of this Study Aid include: revising grammar, revising vocabulary, exam preparation, translation from Spanish, prose composition, comprehension, essay writing, oral tests, dictation, verb tables.

A complete guide to preparing for O level, School Certificate and equivalent examinations in Spanish, written by an experienced teacher and examiner in Spanish.

N. P. O. Green, J. M. Potter and G. W. Stout
Biology £2.50

The contents of this Study Aid include: the cell and organization of life, nutrition, respiration, transport, excretion, temperature regulation, co-ordination, the skeleton and locomotion, reproduction, growth and development, genetics and evolution, ecology, microbiology.

A complete guide to preparing for O level, School Certificate and equivalent examinations in Biology.

PAN STUDY AIDS

R. Warson
Accounts and Book-keeping £1.95

The contents of this Study Aid include: profits and stock, profit and loss, the balance sheet, adjustments, the trial balance, final accounts, the journal, banking and petty cash, VAT, control accounts, receipts and payments, income and expenditure, partnership, limited liability.

A complete guide to preparing for O level, School Certificate and equivalent examinations in Accounting, Booking-keeping and Accounts and any course requiring an introduction to accounting practice.

R. P. Jones and I. Hobday
Commerce £2.50

The contents of this Study Aid include: the structure of industry and commerce, the retail trade, the wholesale and commodity markets, buying and selling, private enterprise, the public sector, transport and communications, international trade, money and banking, the Stock Exchange, insurance.

A complete guide to preparing for O level, School Certificate and equivalent examinations in Commerce.

Brian Catchpole
History 1: British £1.95

The contents of this Study Aid include: British economic and social history 1700–1980 – the beginnings of industrial change, the first industrial nation, from the First World War to the present day; British political history 1760–1980.

A complete guide to preparing for O level, School Certificate and equivalent examinations in British and European History.

Brian Catchpole
History 2: European £1.95

The contents of this Study Aid include: Europe 1789-1914 – the French Revolution and Napoleon, Europe 1815–1849, creation and consolidation of the nation states to *c.* 1870, major themes 1870–1914; Europe and world history 1914–1980 – the First World War and the peace treaties, the Russian Revolutions, between the wars, the Second World War, European and world history since 1945.

Together with *History 1: British*, a complete guide to preparing for O level, School Certificate and equivalent examinations in British and European History.

PAN STUDY AIDS – GCSE

- The complete guide to GCSE exam success
- Authors, highly experienced teachers, examiners and writers in every case, have taken account of ALL syllabuses in their subjects
- GCSE Study Aids cover all the essentials, focusing on the areas which carry the most marks and paying particular attention to common points of difficulty
- GCSE Study Aids supply expert guidance on how to revise and prepare for the exams
- GCSE Study Aids illustrate the varied types of exam questions, explaining exactly what examiners look for
- GCSE Study Aids give students the chance to practise their answers using sample questions supplied by the examination boards.

Books in the series:

GCSE Biology

GCSE Chemistry

GCSE Commerce

GCSE Computer Studies

GCSE Economics

GCSE English Language

GCSE History 1: World History since 1914

GCSE History 2: Britain and Europe since 1700

GCSE Human Biology

GCSE Mathematics

GCSE Physics

GCSE Sociology